Descendants of Peter Garland

Generation 1

1. **PETER**[1] **GARLAND** was born about 1774 in Lunenburg County, Virginia. He died between 09 Oct 1817-03 Nov 1818 in Giles County, Tennessee. He married (1) **MARY REAMEY**, daughter of Daniel Reamey and Mary (unknown) before 1800. She died between 29 Nov 1843-07 Dec 1846 in Chester County, Tennessee. He married (2) **UNKNOWN UNKNOWN** about 1794.

More About Peter Garland:
Military Service: War of 1812 - Virginia

Notes for Peter Garland:
Will dated October 9, 1817.
Will Proven November 3, 1818.
Inventory of Estate taken on November 12, 1818

Will Of Peter Garland

God have mercy on me and in his name I make and ordain this my last will and testament revoking all others I will one third part of all my Estate to my dear Wife and give her all my household and kitchen furniture during her natural life then to be divided between her two daughters Juliana and Maria Luisa The balance of my Estate I wish equally divided between the before mentioned two children and Mrs Alexanders children from Bonaparte Jefferson to Wirter Walt (torn off) all to have an equal proportion -Amen
     9th Oct 1817   (signed) P Garland

Notes for Mary Reamey:
              Will Of Mary Reamey
I Mary Alexander do make and publish this as my last will and Testament hereby revoking and making void all other wills by me at any time made First I direct that my Funeral Expenses and all my debts be paid out of the first moneys that may come in to the hands of my Executor Secondly I give and bequeth unto my son Martin Alexander five dollars Thirdly I give and bequeth unto Greenwood Alexander five dollars   Fourthly I give and bequeth unto Nancy Pace five dollars Fifthly to my son Robert Garland five dollars Sixthly I give unto the heirs of my son Edward Garland five dollars Seventhly I give unto my daughter Francis Pate five dollars Eighthly I give unto my daughter Mary Angus five dollars Ninethly I give and bequeth unto my son Bonapart Garland a certain negroman slave named Joseph Tenthly the balance of all of my Estate to be Equally divided between my sons Bonapart Garland and Peter Garland and Thomas L. Garland and Harriet Wilmot Simmons and John C. Garland and William W. Garland I do hereby nominate and appoint my son William W. Garland as my Executor in witness where of I do to this my will set my hand and seal this the 29th november 1843.
              (signed) Mary Alexander

Signed Sealed and published in our presance and we have subscribed our names hereto in the presance of the Testator
              John C. Vantrease
              William C. Vantrease

Will dated November 29, 1843
Will probated December 7, 1846

Autobiography of Joseph Daniel Garland, her grandson, states Mary is buried in Old Pisgah Cemetery, Chester County, Tennessee.

Peter Garland and Mary Reamey had the following children:

2.   i. MARY C.[2] GARLAND was born about 1795 in Virginia. She died between 09 Jul 1860-18 Aug 1870. She married Alexander Angus in Giles County, Tennessee. He was born about 1791 in Virginia. He died after 18 Aug 1870.

       ii. FRANCES GARLAND was born about 1797 in Henry County, Virginia. She married JOHN PATE.

Notes for Frances Garland:
Possibly a daughter of Thomas Alexander who stayed with her mother when Thomas went to Kentucky.

      iii. BONAPARTE ROBERT GARLAND was born in 1801 in Henry County, Virginia. He died on 16 Aug 1884 in Franklin County, Alabama. He married Amanda W. Gardner, daughter of Theophilus Gardner and Elizabeth (unknown) on 24 Jan 1869 in Tishomingo County, Mississippi. She was born on 24 Jun 1824 in North Carolina. She died on 16 Feb 1901 in Mississippi.

More About Bonaparte Robert Garland:
Burial: Winchester Cemetery, Franklin County, Alabama
Living In: 1850 Living in the household of Joseph Bell in District 6, Franklin County, Alabama
Living In: 1859 in Franklin County, Alabama
Occupation: Bet. 1828-1832; Justice of the Peace in Franklin County, Alabama
Occupation: Bet. 1842-1843; State Representative from Franklin County, Alabama
Occupation: Bet. 1845-1846; State Representative from Tuscaloosa, Alabama
Occupation: Bet. 1847-1848; State Representative from Franklin County, Alabama
Occupation: 1850 in District 6, Franklin County, Alabama; Farmer
Occupation:1870 in Township 6, Range 15, Franklin County, Alabama; Farmer
Occupation:1880 in Franklin County, Alabama; Farmer
Property: 01 Dec 1859 in Purchased Land Offered for Sale by U.S. Government at Huntsville, Alabama; 79 and 87/100 Acres
Property: 1880 in Franklin County, Alabama; 320 Acres (20 tilled and 300 woodland)

      iv. DANIEL REAMEY GARLAND was born about 1802 in Henry County, Virginia. He died before 1841.

More About Daniel Reamey Garland:
Living In: 06 Oct 1840 Franklin County, Alabama
Property: 06 Oct 1840; Purchased land offered for sale by the U.S. Government at Pontotoc, Mississippi: 160 and 80/100 Acres
Property: 06 Oct 1840; Purchased land offered for sale by the U.S. Government at Pontotoc, Mississippi: 160 Acres

      v. ROBERT REAMEY GARLAND was born about 1804 in Henry County, Virginia. He died in Vicksburg, Mississippi.

3.   vi. PETER GARLAND was born on 30 Dec 1805 in Henry County, Virginia. He died on 24 Feb 1873 in Thorp Spring, Hood County, Texas. He married (1) LUCINDA A. GOFF, daughter of Thomas Goff and (unknown) Allen before 1831 in Tennessee. She was born in Tennessee. She died in Mississippi. He married (2) LOUISA PHILLIPS in 1845

in Curdy, Mississippi. She was born on 08 Feb 1828 in Mississippi. She died on 31 Dec 1902 in Chickasha, Chickasha Nation, Indian Territory (present day Oklahoma).

4.   vii.   EDWARD GARLAND was born before 1807 in Henry County, Virginia. He died before 5 Dec 1850. He married (1) NANCY W. SMISER, daughter of John Smiser and Eve Mary Turney on 14 May 1821 in Columbia, Tennessee. She was born about 1805 in Maury County, Tennessee. She died before 1840. He married (2) MARTHA JANE BULLOCK, daughter of Francis Bullock and Rachel Vestal about 1837 in Tennessee. She was born about 1806 in North Carolina. She died on 01 Mar 1875 in Tishomingo County, Mississippi.

5.   viii.   THOMAS LOWERY GARLAND was born on 20 Jul 1807 in Henry County, Virginia. He died on 24 Sep 1868 in White County, Arkansas. He married Saphronia Richardson Hearn, daughter of Isham Green Hearn and Amy Gilliam Harris in 1827 in Madison County, Tennessee. She was born on 15 Jun 1812 in North Carolina. She died on 22 Jul 1858 in Chester County, Tennessee.

6.   ix.   HARRIET WILMOT GARLAND was born on 04 Jul 1810 in Henry County, Virginia. She died on 15 Jul 1859 in Chester County, Tennessee. She married James Martin Simmons, son of Solomon Simmons and Mary (unknown) about 1827 in Giles County, Tennessee. He was born about 1801 in Wake County, North Carolina. He died after 10 Jun 1880.

7.   x.   JOHN CALHOUN GARLAND was born on 12 Dec 1810 in Henry County, Virginia. He died on 02 Sep 1874 in Annona, Texas. He married Nancy Johnson, daughter of Joseph Johnson and (unknown) about 1839 in Montgomery, Tennessee. She was born on 30 May 1815 in North Carolina. She died on 30 Nov 1881 in Annona, Texas. He met (UNKNOWN) GARLAND.

8.   xi.   WILLIAM WIRT GARLAND was born on 15 Aug 1812 in Henry County, Virginia. He died on 06 Jun 1901 in Madison County, Tennessee. He married Elizabeth A. Exum, daughter of John Exum and Martha (unknown) on 15 Jan 1841 in Madison County, Tennessee. She was born in 1818 in Tennessee. She died in 1873 in Tennessee.

Peter Garland and Unknown Unknown had the following children:

    xii.   JULIANA GARLAND was born about 1795.

    xiii.   MARIA LOUISA GARLAND was born about 1797.

Generation 2

2.   MARY C.^{2} GARLAND (Peter^1) was born about 1795 in Virginia. She died between 09 Jul 1860-18 Aug 1870. She married Alexander Angus in Giles County, Tennessee. He was born about 1791 in Virginia. He died after 18 Aug 1870.

Notes for Mary C. Garland:
Possibly a daughter of Thomas Alexander who stayed with her mother when Thomas went to Kentucky.

More About Alexander Angus:
Living In: 1820   Pulaski, Giles County, Tennessee
Living In: 1830   Giles County, Tennessee

Living In: 1840 Madison County, Tennessee
Occupation: 1850 in District 3, Tipton County, Tennessee; Farmer
Occupation: 1860 in District 3, Tipton County, Tennessee; Farmer
Occupation: 1870 in District 3, Tipton County, Tennessee; Farmer

Alexander Angus and Mary C. Garland had the following children:

9.   i. THOMAS L.[3] ANGUS was born about 1825 in Tennessee. He married ELIZABETH (UNKNOWN). She was born about 1823 in South Carolina.

     ii. EDWARD E. ANGUS was born about 1830 in Tennessee.

More About Edward E. Angus:
Living In: 1860 With his parents in Tipton County, Tennessee
Occupation: 1860 - Farmer

     iii. DANIEL ANGUS was born in Jul 1832 in Tennessee. He married NANCY H. (UNKNOWN). She was born in Feb 1849 in Missouri. She died before 05 May 1910.

More About Daniel Angus:
Occupation: 1880 in Kinsley, Edwards County, Kansas; Stable Keeper
Occupation: 1900 in Harrison, Boone County, Arkansas; Liveryman
Occupation: 1910 in Arapahoe County, Colorado; Retired

     iv. AREY E. ANGUS was born about 1834 in Tennessee.

     v. ELIZA J. ANGUS was born about 1837 in Tennessee.

     vi. SARAH F. ANGUS was born about 1839 in Tennessee.

More About Sarah F. Angus:
Living In: 1860 With her parents in Tipton County, Tennessee

3.   **PETER[2] GARLAND** (Peter[1]) was born on 30 Dec 1805 in Henry County, Virginia. He died on 24 Feb 1873 in Thorp Spring, Hood County, Texas. He married (1) **LUCINDA A. GOFF**, daughter of Thomas Goff and (unknown) Allen before 1831 in Tennessee. She was born in Tennessee. She died in Mississippi. He married (2) **LOUISA PHILLIPS** in 1845 in Curdy, Mississippi. She was born on 08 Feb 1828 in Mississippi. She died on 31 Dec 1902 in Chickasha, Chickasha Nation, Indian Territory (present day Oklahoma).

More About Peter Garland:
Burial: Thorp Spring Cemetery, Thorp Spring, Texas
Living In: 1840 Tishomingo County, Mississippi
Living In: 1841 Tishomingo County, Mississippi
Living In: 1845 Tishomingo County, Mississippi
Occupation: Bet. 1842-1843; Deputy Sheriff, Tishomingo County, Mississippi
Occupation: 1850 in Northern Division District 4, Tishomingo County, Mississippi; Farmer
Occupation: 1870 in Hood County, Texas; Farmer
Property: 06 Feb 1860 in Houston and Nacogdoches Land Districts, Henderson County, Texas; With his son, Christopher, purchased 80 acres.
Property: 1869 in Erath County, Texas; With his son, C.C. Garland, 640 Acres.
Property: 21 Dec 1870 in Milam District, Erath County, Texas; With his son, Christopher, purchased 80 acres.

Notes for Peter Garland:

CAPTAIN PETER GARLAND.

FRONTIERSMAN.

by Barbara Thorp Wilkins

Peter and Louisa (Phillips) Garland moved from near Stephenville in Erath County to Hood County in 1860, settling on Stroud's Creek near Thorp Spring. As the Civil War loomed, bloody Comanche raids on the settlers of the frontier area continued and would for another decade, despite removal of all Indian tribes from northern Texas to the reservations of what is now Oklahoma.

Controversy followed the volatile Garland to Hood County, and some historical writers still debate the part he played in the early history of this "wide-open" part of Texas. As a Captain in the Frontier Guard, Garland has alternately been condemned as an "Indian-hater of the first order" and "murderer" and hailed as a fearless Indian fighter, defender of the frontier, leading citizen and hero. In retrospect, out of the context of the times, it is doubtful that controversy will ever be resolved. In his Hood County History, Thomas Ewell commented that Garland was "honored and trusted by the people who knew him best and were personally cognizant of all the events." This must have reflected the views of many of Garland's contemporaries, as he was elected the first Treasurer of Hood County in 1867.

Capt. Peter Garland of Texas was born in 1805 in Henry County, Virginia, the grandson of Col. David Garland of the Revolution and son of Maj. Peter Garland of the Virginia 64th Regiment in the War of 1812. His grandfather and father had wars to fight. Capt. Peter Garland, some say, created his own war, against the Indians of the Texas frontier..

After leaving Virginia, young Garland was first married to Lucinda Goff in Tennessee and second to Louisa Phillips in Mississippi as he traveled the migration route to Texas, fathering a total of at least 12 children. Before coming to Anderson County, Texas, in 1850, Garland was a Deputy Sheriff, Circuit Court Clerk and saloonkeeper in Tishomingo County, Mississippi. In 1857, the Garlands braved the raw frontier of Erath County along with several other families, including the Thorntons, Hightowers and Wylies. Ten years later, in Hood County, Peter and Louisa's 16-year-old daughter, Melissa Virginia, was married to James Goodhope Thorp, eldest son of Pleasant and Nancy Thorp, founders of Thorp Spring. James and Melissa Virginia had nine children, all born in Thorp Spring; and their fourth child was Pleasant Garland Thorp, my grandfather..

Capt. Peter Garland died in 1873 in Thorp Spring and is buried there in the old Thorp Spring Cemetery.

This article was scanned from the Hood County Genealogical Society Newsletter No. 16, dated November 1987, Editor Merle McNeese

---

Peter Garland and Lucinda A. Goff had the following children:

 i. EDWARD[3] GARLAND was born in 1825 in Tennessee.

 ii. THOMAS L. GARLAND was born in 1829 in Tennessee. He married Martha D. Wylie on 03 Oct 1849 in Tishomingo County, Mississippi. She was born about 1831 in

Alabama.

More About Thomas L. Garland:
Occupation: 1860 in Beat 7, Anderson County, Texas; Stock Raising
Occupation: 1870 in Anderson County, Texas; Farmer
Occupation: 1880 in Fincastle, Henderson County, Texas; Farmer

iii. JACK GARLAND was born about 1830 in Tennessee. He died in Bowie, Texas.

10. iv. CHRISTOPHER C. GARLAND was born about 1831 in Tennessee. He married Catherine A. Broach on 24 Jan 1855 in Anderson County, Texas. She was born about 1833 in Tennessee.

11. v. WILLIAM GARLAND was born about 1835 in Tennessee. He married Elizabeth Broach on 24 May 1855 in Harris County, Texas. She was born about 1837 in Tennessee.

12. vi. MARY ANNA GARLAND was born on 26 Jan 1837 in Tennessee. She died on 10 Feb 1906 in Erath County, Texas. She married Daniel Robert Thornton, son of Thomas Thornton and (unknown) Roberts on 27 Jul 1853 in Anderson County, Texas. He was born on 27 Mar 1833 in Alabama. He died on 15 Jun 1911 in Huckabay, Erath County, Texas.

13. vii. LUCINDA GARLAND was born about 1840 in Mississippi. She died after 27 Apr 1910 in Texas. She married Joshua Columbus Hightower, son of Charnell Hightower and Elon Watts on 02 Nov 1855 in Anderson County, Texas. He was born on 21 Mar 1834 in Chickasaw County, Mississippi. He died in 1915 in Hood County, Texas.

viii. JEFFERSON GARLAND was born about 1842 in Mississippi. He died in Stephenville, Texas.

More About Jefferson Garland:
Living In: 1880 Living with his nephew, Columbus Erastus Thornton, in Precinct 7, Erath County, Texas

Notes for Jefferson Garland:
Never Married.

More About Louisa Phillips:
Burial: Rose Hill Cemetery, Chickasha, Oklahoma
Living In: 1880 Precinct 6, Hood County, Texas
Living In: 1900 With her son, Daniel N. Garland, in Chickasha, Chickasha Nation, Indian Territory (present day Oklahoma)

Peter Garland and Louisa Phillips had the following children:
ix. JOSEPH GARLAND was born on 24 Sep 1847 in Farrington, Mississippi.

14. x. MELISSA VIRGINIA GARLAND was born on 03 May 1851 in Henderson County, Texas. She died on 25 Oct 1928 in Brownwood, Texas. She married James Goodhope Thorp, son of Pleasant Earl Thorp and Nancy Hicks Oldham on 03 Apr 1867 in Hood County, Texas. He was born on 30 Mar 1845 in Burleson County, Texas. He died on 13 Oct 1915 in Thorp Spring, Texas.

xi.   ALLISON NELSON GARLAND was born on 28 Oct 1859 in Stephenville, Texas. He died on 27 Mar 1891 in Lehigh, Coal County, Indian Terrirtory (present day Oklahoma). He married Mollie Wright on 13 Mar 1889 in Hood County, Texas.

More About Allison Nelson Garland:
Burial: Lehigh cemetery, Lehigh, Coal County, Indian Territory (present day Oklahoma)

15.   xii. SUSAN AVARILLA GARLAND was born on 20 Feb 1854 in Anderson County, Texas. She died on 02 Aug 1920 in Granbury, Texas. She married David Lee Nutt, son of David Nutt and Sarah Lee Landers on 28 Feb 1872 in Thorp Spring, Texas. He was born on 06 Jan 1848 in Neosha, Missouri. He died on 18 Feb 1929 in Granbury, Texas.

xiii.   ALMARINE ALEXANDER GARLAND was born on 02 Jun 1856 in Texas. He died on 18 Apr 1869 in Texas.

More About Almarine Alexander Garland:
Burial: Thorp Spring Cemetery, Thorp Spring, Texas

Notes   for   Almarine   Alexander
Garland:
Killed by a horse.

16.   xiv. DANIEL N. GARLAND was born on 09 Apr 1864 in Thorp Spring, Hood County, Texas. He died on 28 Nov 1921 in Marlin, Texas. He married Inez Caldwell Toole, daughter of Alfred Toole and Belinda Yates on 18 Jan 1888 in Canadian, Choctaw Nation, Indian Territory (present day Canadian, Oklahoma). She was born on 26 May 1864 in Alabama. She died on 08 Apr 1931 in Dallas, Texas.

xv.   MARTHA OLIVE GARLAND was born on 01 Jun 1868 in Texas. She died on 08 Mar 1888 in Chickasha, Chickasha Nation, Indian Territory (present day Oklahoma). She married Jack C. Brown on 19 May 1887 in Granbury, Texas.

4.   EDWARD[2] GARLAND (Peter[1]) was born before 1807 in Henry County, Virginia. He died before 05 Dec 1850. He married (1) **NANCY W. SMISER**, daughter of John Smiser and Eve Mary Turney on 14 May 1821 in Columbia, Tennessee. She was born about 1805 in Maury County, Tennessee. She died before 1840. He married (2) **MARTHA JANE BULLOCK**, daughter of Francis Bullock and Rachel Vestal about 1837 in Tennessee. She was born about 1806 in North Carolina. She died on 01 Mar 1875 in Tishomingo County, Mississippi.

Notes for Nancy W. Smiser:
Selina, Eliza and Mary were raised by their grandparents, John Smiser and Eve Mary Turney Smiser after about 1830.

Edward Garland and Nancy W. Smiser had the following children:

17.   i. SALINA J.[3] GARLAND was born in Feb 1823 in Tennessee. She died in Dec 1903 in Denver, Colorado. She married Claudius Buchanan Hall, son of Thomas James Hall and Emma Wallace on 20 Nov 1845 in Maury County, Tennessee. He was born on 21 Jan 1820 in Tennessee. He died between 05 Sep 1870-07 Jun 1880.

18.   ii. EDWARD WARREN GARLAND was born on 28 Oct 1825 in Giles County, Tennessee. He died on 12 May 1897 in Texas. He married (1) JULIA REBECCA KIMBELL, daughter of John M. Kimbell and Sarah Angelina Elliott before 1878. She was born on 31 Mar

1845 in the Republic of Texas. She died on 26 Jan 1908 in Texas. He married (2) MARY EMELINE JENKINS, daughter of James Wilson Jenkins and Sarah Dowd on 18 Jun 1845 in Tishomingo County, Mississippi. She was born on 25 Oct 1827 in Chatham County, North Carolina. She died on 21 Feb 1887 in Hardin County, Tennessee.

    iii.   ELLEN GARLAND was born about 1829 in Tennessee.

        More About Ellen Garland:
        Living In: 1850 Living in the household of Mary Booker in Maury County, Tennessee.

    iv.   MARY GARLAND.

    v.   ELIZA GARLAND.

More About Martha Jane Bullock:
Living In: 1855 Franklin County, Alabama
Living In: 1860 Franklin County, Alabama
Living In: 1870 Tishomingo County, Mississippi with her husband, Jonathan Winchester
Occupation: 1850 in Franklin County, Alabama; Farmer

Edward Garland and Martha Jane Bullock had the following children:

    vi.   ROBERT W. GARLAND was born about 1838 in Alabama. He died on 31 Dec 1862 in Murfreesboro, Tennessee.

        More About Robert W. Garland:
        Living In: 1860 Living in the household of his mother in Franklin County, Alabama.
        Occupation: 1860 in Franklin County, Alabama; Farmer
        Military Service: Bet. 15 Jul 1861-31 Dec 1862; Company H, 16th Alabama Infantry, C.S.A.

        Notes for Robert W. Garland:
        Enlisted in Company H, 16th Alabama Infantry on July 15, 1861 at Tuscumbia, Colbert County, Alabama.
        Killed in action December 31, 1862 at Murfreesboro, Tennessee.

    vii.   JOHN J. GARLAND was born about 1841 in Alabama.

        More About John J. Garland:
        Living In: 1860 With his uncle, William Bullock, in Franklin County, Alabama
        Occupation: 1860 in Franklin County, Alabama; Farm Labor

19.   viii. RACHEL ANN GARLAND was born on 04 Oct 1844 in Henderson County, Tennessee. She died on 23 Aug 1929 in Franklin County, Alabama. She married Richard L. Winchester, son of Jonathan Winchester and Sarah Bruzil on 10 Feb 1867 in Pleasant Site, Franklin County, Alabama. He was born on 17 Feb 1839 in Heard County, Georgia. He died on 30 Jun 1919 in Pleasant Site, Franklin County, Alabama.

20.   ix.   MARTHA ANN GARLAND was born on 29 Sep 1849 in Mississippi. She died on 08 Jan

1877 in Tishomingo County, Mississippi. She married Francis Marion Winchester, son of Jonathan Winchester and Ellenor Glover in Oct 1869. He was born in Jun 1849 in Mississippi. He died after 28 Apr 1910 in Texas.

5.   **THOMAS LOWERY**[2] **GARLAND** (Peter[1]) was born on 20 Jul 1807 in Henry County, Virginia. He died on 24 Sep 1868 in White County, Arkansas. He married Saphronia Richardson Hearn, daughter of Isham Green Hearn and Amy Gilliam Harris in 1827 in Madison County, Tennessee. She was born on 15 Jun 1812 in North Carolina. She died on 22 Jul 1858 in Chester County, Tennessee.

More About Thomas Lowery Garland:
Burial: Old Pisgah Cemetery, Chester County, Tennessee
Living In: 01 May 1861 in White County, Arkansas
Occupation: 1850 in Madison County, Tennessee; Farmer
Occupation: 1860 in near Bradford, White County, Arkansas;
Farmer
Occupation: Methodist Minister
Property: 01 May 1861; Purchased 80 acres from land offered for sale by U.S. Government at Batesville, Arkansas.

Notes for Thomas Lowery Garland:
Autobiography of Joseph D. Garland gives birthdate as April 20, 1807. Headstone shows July 20, 1807. Autobiography gives death date as September 20, 1868. Headstone gives death date as September 24, 1868.

More About Saphronia Richardson Hearn:
Burial: Hearn Chapel Cemetery, Chester County, Tennessee

Thomas Lowery Garland and Saphronia Richardson Hearn had the following children:

21.   i. MARTHA A. ELIZABETH[3] GARLAND was born on 23 Nov 1829 in Madison County, Tennessee. She died on 07 May 1918 in Little Rock, Pulaski County, Arkansas. She married John Leemona Walsh, son of Johnathan Walsh and Winifred Kirby on 30 Nov 1856 in Madison County, Tennessee. He was born about 1825 in Tennessee. He died on 25 Mar 1885.

   ii. JOHN CRAWLEY GARLAND was born on 15 Mar 1832 in Madison County, Tennessee. He died in Sep 1884 in Woodruff County, Arkansas. He married Mary E. Slaughter on 12 Apr 1868 in Tipton County, Tennessee. She was born on 08 May 1850 in Madison County, Tennessee. She died on 14 Feb 1899 in Woodruff County, Arkansas.

   More About John Crawley Garland:
   Burial: Augusta Memorial Park, Augusta, Woodruff County, Arkansas
   Occupation: 1860 in Union, White County, Arkansas; M. D.
   Occupation: 1870 in Covington, Tipton County, Tennessee; Druggist
   Occupation: 1880 in Augusta, Woodruff County, Arkansas; Physician
   Military Service: Company A, 36th Arkansas Infantry, C.S.A.

   Notes for John Crawley Garland:
       Lost a leg due to being hit by a cannon ball in battle of Helena, Arkansas July 4, 1863. Captured and sent to Memphis General Hospital in Memphis, Tennessee on U.S. hospital steamer "R.C. Wood". Sent from Officers Hospital in Memphis, Tennessee to prisoner of war camp at Johnson Island, Ohio on April 18, 1864. Arrived at Johnson Island on April 26, 1864 and was transferred to Fortress Monroe

for exchange on September 16, 1864. Injury confirmed by C.S.A. surgeon on September 26, 1864.

Enlisted on June 14, 1862 at Searcy, Arkansas. Mustered in June 24, 1862 at Springfield, Arkansas.

Promoted from first lieutenant to captain on November 5, 1862.

22.   iii. WILLIAM WIRT GARLAND was born on 03 Jan 1835 in Madison County, Tennessee. He died in 1908 in Conway County, Arkansas. He married Mary Elizabeth McKnight on 19 Dec 1854 in Madison County, Tennessee. She was born in Aug 1836 in Tennessee. She died in 1914 in Conway County, Arkansas.

    iv. ISHAM GREEN GARLAND was born on 06 Jan 1837 in Madison County, Tennessee. He died on 11 Aug 1870 in Augusta, Arkansas. He married Lou Shelly in Jackson County, Arkansas.

More About Isham Green Garland:
Burial: Augusta Memorial Park, Augusta, Woodruff County, Arkansas
Occupation: 1860 in Glaize Township, Jackson County, Arkansas; Dry Goods Clerk
Occupation: Merchant
Military Service: Company E, 46th Arkansas Cavalry, C.S.A.

    v. THOMAS LOWERY GARLAND was born on 21 Feb 1839 in Madison County, Tennessee. He died on 19 Aug 1883 in Hood County, Texas.

More About Thomas Lowery Garland: Burial:
Granbury Cemetery, Granbury, Texas
Living In: 1880 Living with his first cousin, Susan Avarilla Garland, and her family in Granbury, Hood County, Texas.
Occupation: 1880 in Granbury, Hood County, Texas; Working in Livery Stable
Occupation: Merchant
Military Service: 07 May 1861 in Enlisted in McCulloch's First Texas Cavalry, C.S.A., at Camp Cooper, Texas
Notes for Thomas Lowery
Garland: Never Married
Served in Company G, McCulloch's First Texas Cavalry, Company G, Taylor's 8th Battalion of Texas Cavalry and Company G of Yager's First Texas Cavalry.

23.   vi. ROBERT REAMEY GARLAND was born on 07 Jan 1841 in Madison County, Tennessee. He died on 08 Oct 1923 in Emmet, Nevada County, Arkansas. He married Hannah Josephine McSwain on 10 Sep 1865 in Columbia County, Arkansas. She was born on 30 Aug 1848 in Marshall County, Mississippi. She died on 16 Jun 1915 in Emmet, Nevada County, Arkansas.

24.   vii. JOSEPH DANIEL GARLAND was born on 21 Apr 1843 in Madison County, Tennessee. He died on 05 Jan 1918 in Polk County, Arkansas. He married Zuritha Ann Parrish on 09 Aug 1866 in Grand Glaze, Jackson County, Arkansas. She was born on 01 Jan 1843 in Tipton County, Tennessee. She died in Jan 1927.

    viii. SARAH HEARN GARLAND was born on 08 Aug 1847 in Tennessee. She died on 12 Dec 1881 in White County, Arkansas. She married CALLIER ADKIN STEED. He was born on 28 Jan 1843. He died on 20 May 1920 in White County, Arkansas.

More About Sarah Hearn Garland:
Burial: Carter Cemetery, Russell, White County, Arkansas
Living In: 1860 Living with her sister, Martha, and her family in District 4, Hardin County, Tennessee.

6.   **HARRIET WILMOT**[2] **GARLAND** (Peter[1]) was born on 04 Jul 1810 in Henry County, Virginia. She died on 15 Jul 1859 in Chester County, Tennessee. She married James Martin Simmons, son of Solomon Simmons and Mary (unknown) about 1827 in Giles County, Tennessee. He was born about 1801 in Wake County, North Carolina. He died after 10 Jun 1880.

More About Harriet Wilmot Garland:
Burial: Old Pisgah Cemetery, Chester County, Tennessee
Living In: 1850 District 1, Madison County, Tennessee with her children.

Notes for Harriet Wilmot Garland:
Will probated September 1, 1859 in Madison County, Tennessee.

More About James Martin Simmons:
Living In: 1850 In the home of his brother , Britton Simmons, in District 12, Giles County, Tennessee
Living In: 1860 In the home of his nephew, James Simmons, in Northern Subdivision, Giles County, Tennessee
Living In: 1880 Living with his daughter, Martha, and her husband, Joseph A. Davis, in District 1, Madison County, Tennessee.
Occupation: Farmer in 1850

James Martin Simmons and Harriet Wilmot Garland had the following children:

     i.   SOLOMON B.[3] SIMMONS was born on 26 Jan 1828 in Giles County, Tennessee.

26.   ii. JAMES MARTIN SIMMONS was born on 05 Dec 1830 in Madison County, Tennessee. He died on 26 Nov 1912 in Henderson County, Tennessee. He married (1) MARY ELIZABETH CHESSIER on 18 Mar 1856. She was born on 11 Mar 1836 in Halifax, Virginia. She died on 01 Aug 1896 in Henderson County, Tennessee. He married (2) ANNA H. (UNKNOWN) about 1897. She was born in Feb 1862 in Mississippi.

27.   iii. PETER GARLAND SIMMONS was born on 15 Oct 1832 in Madison County, Tennessee. He died before 11 Jul 1915. He married Anna Elizabeth Chesser, daughter of William Chesser and Lon Muse on 10 Sep 1857 in Madison County, Tennessee. She was born on 11 Mar 1837 in Virginia. She died on 11 Jul 1915 in Henderson, Chester County, Tennessee.

28.   iv. MARTHA JANE SIMMONS was born on 16 Nov 1833 in Madison County, Tennessee. She died on 25 Apr 1890. She married (1) JOHN W. BROWDER on 05 Sep 1853 in Madison County, Tennessee. He was born on 12 Sep 1824 in Virginia. He died after 13 Sep 1866. She married JOSEPH A. DAVIS. He was born on 29 Apr 1830 in Virginia. He died on 18 Oct 1902.

    v.   WILLIAM WIRT SIMMONS was born on 20 Jan 1836 in Madison County, Tennessee.

28.   vi. MARY FRANCES SIMMONS was born on 15 Apr 1839 in Madison County, Tennessee. She died on 16 May 1921 in Henderson, Chester County, Tennessee. She married Edward L. Sanford on 23 Dec 1857 in Madison County, Tennessee. He was born about 1837 in Tennessee. He died in 1897.

29. vii. JOHN CRAWLEY SIMMONS was born on 03 Jan 1841 in Madison County, Tennessee. He died on 10 Feb 1911 in Henderson, Chester County, Tennessee. He married Rebecca L. Garland, daughter of William Wirt Garland and Elizabeth A. Exum on 22 Oct 1867 in Madison County, Tennessee. She was born on 28 Oct 1847 in Chester County, Tennessee. She died on 07 Apr 1921 in Civil District 6, Chester County, Tennessee.

30. viii. NANCY WILMOT SIMMONS was born on 03 Jan 1843 in Madison County, Tennessee. She died on 09 Feb 1894 in Annona, Texas. She married Thomas Crutcher Holt on 02 Feb 1862 in Holly Springs, Mississippi. He was born on 01 May 1833 in Tennessee. He died on 11 Nov 1909 in Annona, Texas.

ix. LUCINDA SOPHRENIA SIMMONS was born on 16 Jun 1845 in Madison County, Tennessee.

x. ALMARINE ALEXANDER SIMMONS was born on 27 Jan 1847 in Madison County, Tennessee.

Notes for Almarine Alexander Simmons:
1850 U.S. census gives sex as female. Harriet's brother, Peter Garland, had a son named Almarine Alexander Garland. If Almarine Simmons is a male there is a marriage record of Almarine A. Simmons to Fannie E. Franklin on November 14, 1867 in Madison County, Tennessee.

7. **JOHN CALHOUN^2 GARLAND** (Peter^1) was born on 12 Dec 1810 in Henry County, Virginia. He died on 2 Sep 1874 in Annona, Texas. He married Nancy Johnson, daughter of Joseph Johnson and (unknown) about 1839 in Montgomery, Tennessee. She was born on 30 May 1815 in North Carolina. She died on 30 Nov 1881 in Annona, Texas. He met (UNKNOWN) GARLAND.

More About John Calhoun Garland: Burial:
Garland Cemetery, Annona, Texas
Occupation: 1850 in disrict 3, McNairy County, Tennessee; Farmer
Occupation: 1860 in Beat 3, Bowie County, Texas; Farmer
Occupation: 1870 in Precinct 3, Red River County, Texas; Farmer
Property: 1870 in Red River County, Texas; 240 Acres Improved and 4300 Acres Unimproved

More About Nancy Johnson:
Burial: Garland Cemetery, Annona, Texas
Living In: 1880 Living with her daughter, Mary, and family in Red River County, Texas

John Calhoun Garland and Nancy Johnson had the following children:
i. MARY C.^{3} GARLAND was born on 25 Jan 1835 in Madison County, Tennessee. She died on 30 Dec 1913 in Annona, Texas. She married James W. Sloan, son of Shumate J. Sloan and Elizabeth (Unknown) about 1878 in Madison County, Tennessee. He was born in Dec 1847 in Cherokee County, Alabama. He died on 02 Jan 1914 in Paris, Lamar County, Texas.

More About Mary C. Garland:
Burial: Garland Cemetery, Red River County, Texas
Living In: 1870 Living with her parents in Precinct 3, Red River County, Texas

31. ii. MARGARET C. GARLAND was born on 13 Apr 1838 in Madison County, Tennessee.

She died on 23 Dec 1911 in Annona, Texas. She married Nimrod B. Winston on 17 Sep 1856 in Madison County, Tennessee. He was born on 04 Jan 1836 in Tennessee. He died on 29 Jul 1903 in Annona, Texas.

32. iii. JOSEPH DANIEL RAMEY GARLAND was born on 23 Jun 1840 in Montgomery, Tennessee. He died on 21 Apr 1914 in Annona, Texas. He married (1) JESSIE S. LATIMER, daughter of Henry Russell Latimer and Lucinda Lou Shelton on 27 Oct 1873 in Red River County, Texas. She was born on 06 Feb 1853 in Texas. She died on 06 Jul 1895 in Annona, Texas. He married (2) AVIS IDELLA AGNES SHELTON, daughter of Eli Jenway Shelton and Martha Ann Elizabeth Yates on 23 Nov 1897 in Lamar County, Texas. She was born on 12 Jan 1857 in Lamar County, Texas. She died on 22 Nov 1935 in Nacogdoches, Texas.

John Calhoun Garland and (unknown) Garland had the following child:

33. iv. RUTH GARLAND. She married JAMES GARLAND. He was born about 1800.

8. **WILLIAM WIRT^2 GARLAND** (Peter^1) was born on 15 Aug 1812 in Henry County, Virginia. He died on 6 Jun 1901 in Madison County, Tennessee. He married Elizabeth A. Exum, daughter of John Exum and Martha (unknown) on 15 Jan 1841 in Madison County, Tennessee. She was born in 1818 in Tennessee. She died in 1873 in Tennessee.

More About William Wirt Garland:
Occupation: 1850 in Madison County, Tennessee; Farmer
Occupation: 1860 in Madison County, Tennessee; Farmer
Occupation: 1870 in Madison County, Tennessee; Farmer
Occupation: 1880 in Madison County, Tennessee; Farmer
Occupation: 1900 in Chester County, Tennessee; Farmer
Property: 1850 in Madison County, Tennessee; 200 Acres Improved and 900 Acres Unimproved
Property: 1870 in Madison County, Tennessee; 150 Acres Improved and 700 Acres Unimproved
Property: 1880 in Madison County, Tennessee; 300 Acres Improved and 840 Acres Unimproved

More About William Wirt Garland and Elizabeth A. Exum:
Marriage License: 13 Jan 1841 in Madison County, Tennessee

William Wirt Garland and Elizabeth A. Exum had the following children:

  i. MINERVA^3 GARLAND was born on 28 Jan 1843 in Chester County, Tennessee. She died on 09 Mar 1916 in Henderson, Chester County, Tennessee.

  More About Minerva Garland:
  Burial: 10 Mar 1916 in Garland Cemetery, Henderson, Tennessee
  Cause Of Death: Acute Toxic Gastritis
  Living In: 1870 With her parents in Madison County, Tennessee.
  Living In: 1880 With her father in Madison County, Tennessee.
  Living In: 1900 With her father in Chester County, Tennessee.
  Living In:1910 With her brother, Felix, in Civil District 6, Chester County, Tennessee

  Notes for Minerva
  Garland: Never married.

34. ii. REBECCA L. GARLAND was born on 28 Oct 1847 in Chester County, Tennessee. She died on 07 Apr 1921 in Civil District 6, Chester County, Tennessee. She married John Crawley Simmons, son of James Martin Simmons and Harriet Wilmot Garland

on 22 Oct 1867 in Madison County, Tennessee. He was born on 03 Jan 1841 in Madison County, Tennessee. He died on 10 Feb 1911 in Henderson, Chester County, Tennessee.

iii.   MARTHA E. GARLAND was born on 16 May 1849 in Chester County, Tennessee. She died on 16 May 1914 in Henderson, Chester County, Tennessee. She married Thomas J. McMaster about 1890. He was born on 12 Mar 1840 in Tennessee. He died on 04 Mar 1919 in Henderson, Chester County, Tennessee.

More About Martha E. Garland:
Burial: 17 May 1914 in Henderson, Chester County, Tennessee Cause Of Death: Dysentery
Living In: 1870 With her parents in Madison County, Tennessee.
Living In: 1880 iWith her father in Madison County, Tennessee.

iv.   MARGARET GARLAND was born about Feb 1850. She died on 03 Dec 1923 in Union City, Obion County, Tennessee. She married Joseph W. Temple about 1887. He was born in May 1841 in Tennessee. He died between 11 Jun 1900-02 May 1910.

More About Margaret Garland:
Burial: 04 Dec 1923 in East View Cemetery, Union City, Obion County, Tennessee
Cause Of Death: Carcinoma of Stomach
Living In: 1880 With her father in Madison County, Tennessee.
Living In: 1910 Union City, Obion County, Tennessee
Living In: 1920 Union City, Obion County, Tennessee

35.   v. FELIX EXUM GARLAND was born in Apr 1854 in Chester County, Tennessee. He died on 29 Mar 1912 in Henderson county, Tennessee. He married Nannie Deaton, daughter of John Deaton and Jane Clemmons about 1908. She was born in May 1877 in Tennessee.

vi.   JOHN P. GARLAND was born on 12 Aug 1856 in Tennessee. He died on 16 Apr 1932 in Chester County, Tennessee. He married Alice Kroger, daughter of John Kroger and Margaret Shafer on 28 Nov 1894 in Obion County, Tennessee. She was born on 22 Aug 1867 in Tennessee. She died on 04 Aug 1938 in Henderson, Chester County, Tennessee.

More About John P. Garland:
Burial: 17 Apr 1932 in Garland Cemetery, Henderson, Tennessee
Living In: 1880 Living with his father in Madison County, Tennessee
Occupation: 1880 in Madison County, Tennessee; Farmer
Occupation: 1900 in Civil district 6, Chester County, Tennessee; Farmer
Occupation: 1910 in Civil district 6, Chester County, Tennessee; Farmer
Occupation: 1920 in Jackson Ward 4, Madison County, Tennessee; Farmer

Generation 3

9.   THOMAS L.[3] ANGUS (Mary C.[2] Garland, Peter[1] Garland) was born about 1825 in Tennessee. He married ELIZABETH (UNKNOWN). She was born about 1823 in South Carolina.

More About Thomas L. Angus:
Occupation: 1850 in District 8, Tipton County, Tennessee; Farmer

Thomas L. Angus and Elizabeth (unknown) had the following child:

    i.   JAMES A.[4] ANGUS was born about 1848 in Tennessee.

10.   **CHRISTOPHER C.**[3] **GARLAND** (Peter[2], Peter[1]) was born about 1831 in Tennessee. He married Catherine A. Broach on 24 Jan 1855 in Anderson County, Texas. She was born about 1833 in Tennessee.

More About Christopher C. Garland:
Living In: 1850 With his cousin, Edward Warren Garland, in Northern Division District 4, Tishomingo County, Mississippi
Occupation: 1850 in Tishomingo County, Mississippi; Merchant
Occupation: 1860 in Precinct 2, Limestone County, Texas;
Farmer
Occupation: 1870 in Limestone County, Texas; Planter
Property: 1870 in Limestone County, Texas; 140 Acres Improved and 980 Acres Unimproved

Christopher C. Garland and Catherine A. Broach had the following children:

    i.   PETER[4] GARLAND was born about 1856 in Texas.

    ii.   MADORA GARLAND was born about 1859 in Texas.

11.   **WILLIAM**[3] **GARLAND** (Peter[2], Peter[1]) was born about 1835 in Tennessee. He married Elizabeth Broach on 24 May 1855 in Harris County, Texas. She was born about 1837 in Tennessee.

More About Elizabeth Broach:
Living In: 1870 Elizabeth and her son, George, are living with her brother in law Christopher Garland in Limestone County, Texas

William Garland and Elizabeth Broach had the following child:

    i.   GEORGE T.[4] GARLAND was born about 1857 in Texas.

12.   **MARY ANNA**[3] **GARLAND** (Peter[2], Peter[1]) was born on 26 Jan 1837 in Tennessee. She died on 10 Feb 1906 in Erath County, Texas. She married Daniel Robert Thornton, son of Thomas Thornton and (unknown) Roberts on 27 Jul 1853 in Anderson County, Texas. He was born on 27 Mar 1833 in Alabama. He died on 15 Jun 1911 in Huckabay, Erath County, Texas.

More About Mary Anna Garland:
Burial: Hannibal Cemetery, Hannibal, Erath County,
Texas Cause Of Death: Paralysis of Heart

More About Daniel Robert Thornton:
Burial: 16 Jun 1911 in Hannibal Cemetery, Hannibal, Erath County,
Texas Cause Of Death: Chronic Dysentery
Living In: 1860 Living on the property of Peter Davidson in Palo Pinto County, Texas
Living In: 1911 Corpus Christi, Texas
Occupation: 1860 in Precinct 5, Palo Pinto County, Texas; Stock Raiser
Occupation: 1870 in Willow Spring on Bosque Creek, Erath County, Texas; Stock Raiser
Occupation: 1880 in Precinct 7, Erath County, Texas; Farmer
Occupation: 1900 in Justice Precinct 7, Erath County, Texas;
Farmer
Military Service: Company D, 15th Texas Cavalry, C.S.A.

Notes for Daniel Robert Thornton:
Served as a sergeant in Company D, 15th Texas Cavalry, C.S.A.

Headstone has June 14, 1911 as date of death. Death certificate has June 15, 1911 as date of death.

Daniel Robert Thornton and Mary Anna Garland had the following children:

36.   i. COLUMBUS ERASTUS[4] THORNTON was born on 23 Dec 1855 in Anderson County, Texas. He died on 20 Apr 1937 in Spur, Texas. He married MARY J. CRAWFORD. She was born about 1857 in Arkansas.

37.   ii. THOMAS PETER THORNTON was born on 27 May 1857 in Dripping Springs, Texas. He died on 29 Jan 1917 in Stephenville, Erath County, Texas. He married PARCINDA GORDON. She was born on 06 Apr 1861 in Tyler, Texas. She died on 22 May 1941 in Erath County, Texas.

38.   iii. ELIZABETH LUCINDA THORNTON was born on 29 Aug 1859 in Texas. She died on 15 Mar 1948 in San Angelo, Texas. She married HENRY C. WYLIE.

39.   iv. HENRY CLAY THORNTON was born on 09 Sep 1865 in Erath County, Texas. He died on 27 Sep 1930 in McKinney, Texas. He married Frances Bell Kenny on 05 Aug 1885.

40.   v. WILLIAM LUTHER THORNTON was born on 11 Dec 1866 in Erath County, Texas. He died on 29 Mar 1928 in Breckenridge, Texas. He married JACKIE MAY KENNEDY. She was born on 29 Dec 1871 in Anderson, Texas. She died on 06 Jul 1956 in Sherman, Texas.

    vi. ANNAH N. THORNTON was born on 26 Jan 1869 in Texas. She died on 06 May 1883 in Texas.

      More About Annah N. Thornton:
      Burial: Hannibal Cemetery, Hannibal, Erath County, Texas

41.   vii. ARTHUR E. THORNTON was born on 30 Sep 1871 in Texas. He died on 02 May 1951 in Ralls, Crosby County, Texas. He married Fannie Fulkerson on 27 Nov 1891.

    viii. OSCAR E. THORNTON was born on 30 Sep 1871 in Texas. He died on 14 Aug 1884.

      More About Oscar E. Thornton:
      Burial: Hannibal Cemetery, Hannibal, Erath County, Texas

42.   ix. DANIEL ROBERT THORNTON was born on 09 Jul 1875 in Hannibal, Erath County, Texas. He died on 12 Nov 1959 in Wharton, Wharton County, Texas. He married (1) MARGUERITE V. BASS on 03 Aug 1898. She died in 1918. He married ETHEL RUTH (UNKNOWN).

43.   x. MINNIE KATHLEEN THORNTON was born on 12 Apr 1877 in Erath County, Texas. She died on 28 Jun 1968 in San Antonio, Texas. She married WILLIAM EVERETT WRIGHT. He was born on 20 Mar 1866 in Tennessee. He died on 18 Sep 1946 in San Antonio, Texas.

    xi. (UNKNOWN) THORNTON was born on 15 Jan 1881 in Texas. She died on 15 Jan 1881 in Texas.

13. LUCINDA[3] GARLAND (Peter[2], Peter[1]) was born about 1840 in Mississippi. She died after 27 Apr 1910 in Texas. She married Joshua Columbus Hightower, son of Charnell Hightower and Elon Watts on 02 Nov 1855 in Anderson County, Texas. He was born on 21 Mar 1834 in Chickasaw County, Mississippi. He died in 1915 in Hood County, Texas.

More About Joshua Columbus Hightower:
Living In: 1870 Hood County, Texas
Living In: 1910 Alamogordo, New Mexico
Occupation: 1860 in Johnson County, Texas; Farmer
Occupation: 1880 in Precinct 6, Hood County, Texas; laborer
Occupation: 1900 in Township 14, Creek Nation, Indian Territory (present day Oklahoma); Farmer
Occupation: 1867 - 1873 Sheriff of Hood County, Texas

Notes for Joshua Columbus Hightower:
Joshua is listed as an invalid in the 1910 U.S. census.

Joshua Columbus Hightower and Lucinda Garland had the following children:

  i. WILLIAM ALLEN[4] HIGHTOWER was born in 1857 in Henderson County, Texas.

  ii. MARTHA MARIANNA HIGHTOWER was born on 08 Sep 1859 in Granbury, Texas. She married HENRY ELLIS NESOM.

  iii. JOHN THOMAS HIGHTOWER was born in Mar 1864 in Johnson County, Texas. He married Lydia (unknown) about 1890. She was born in Jan 1870 in Indian Territory (present day Oklahoma).

   More About John Thomas Hightower:
   Living In: 1900 John and his wife are living with his parents in Township 14, Creek Nation, Indian Territory (present day Oklahoma)

  iv. PETER HIGHTOWER was born in 1866 in Hood County, Texas.

  v. SANFORD HIGHTOWER was born in 1868 in Hood County, Texas.

  vi. SUSAN HIGHTOWER was born in 1871 in Hood County, Texas.

44. vii. DELLA HIGHTOWER was born in Jan 1878 in Hood County, Texas. She married (UNKNOWN) MCKIERMAN.

  viii. PEARL HIGHTOWER was born in 1879 in Hood County, Texas.

14. MELISSA VIRGINIA[3] GARLAND (Peter[2], Peter[1]) was born on 03 May 1851 in Henderson County, Texas. She died on 25 Oct 1928 in Brownwood, Texas. She married James Goodhope Thorp, son of Pleasant Earl Thorp and Nancy Hicks Oldham on 03 Apr 1867 in Hood County, Texas. He was born on 30 Mar 1845 in Burleson County, Texas. He died on 13 Oct 1915 in Thorp Spring, Texas.

More About Melissa Virginia Garland:
Burial: 26 Oct 1928 in Thorp Spring Cemetery, Thorp Spring, Texas Cause Of Death: Fractured Hip

More About James Goodhope Thorp:

Burial: Thorp Spring Cemetery, Thorp Spring, Texas
Occupation: 1880 in Precinct 6, Hood County, Texas; Retail Grocer
Occupation: 1900 in Justice Precinct 6, Hood County, Texas; unknown
Occupation: 1910 in Justice Precinct 1, Hood County, Texas; Farmer

James Goodhope Thorp and Melissa Virginia Garland had the following children:

    i. JOHN HENRY [4] THORP was born on 08 Dec 1867 in Hood County, Texas. He died on 30 Oct 1935 in Thorp Springs, Texas.

More About John Henry Thorp:
Burial: 31 Oct 1935 in Thorp Springs, Texas
Living In: 1910 Living with his parents in Justice Precinct 1, Hood County, Texas
Occupation: Farmer

    ii. EULA LEE THORP was born on 17 Feb 1868. She died on 17 Dec 1880.

More About Eula Lee Thorp:
Burial: Thorp Spring Cemetery, Thorp Spring, Texas

    iii. IDA ELIZABETH THORP was born on 08 Dec 1871 in Thorp Spring, Texas. She died on 27 Oct 1912 in Tolar, Hood County, Texas. She married John Andrews on 06 Sep 1893 in Thorpe Spring, Texas.

More About Ida Elizabeth Thorp:
Burial: 28 Oct 1912 in Thorp Springs,
Texas Cause Of Death: Pellagra

45.   iv. PLEASANT GARLAND THORP was born on 14 Mar 1874 in Thorp Spring, Texas. He died on 19 Aug 1946 in Granbury, Texas. He married (1) LOUISA M. ARRINGTON about 1900. She was born on 12 Feb 1881 in Texas. She died on 06 Jan 1978 in Hood County, Texas.

    v. NANNIE LOU THORP was born on 08 Mar 1879. She died on 14 Apr 1894.

    vi. SUSAN OLLIE THORP was born on 30 Jan 1880. She died in Oct 1889 in Hood County, Texas.

More About Susan Ollie Thorp:
Burial: Thorp Spring Cemetery, Thorp Spring, Texas

    vii. JAMES NELSON THORP was born on 26 May 1881. He died on 24 Jan 1883.

More About James Nelson Thorp:
Burial: Thorp Spring Cemetery, Thorp Spring, Texas

46.   viii. LUCY B. THORP was born on 16 Dec 1883 in Texas. She died on 31 Dec 1978 in Bryan, Brazos County, Texas. She married Warner L. Thomas on 08 Sep 1902.

    ix. DANIEL NEWTON THORP was born on 15 May 1886 in Texas. He died on 08 Mar 1965 in Richland Hills, Tarrant County, Texas. He married Coye Mary Light,

daughter of L. E. Light about 1907. She was born on 10 Dec 1889 in
Tennessee. She died on 13 Jul 1978 in Bedford, Tarrant County, Texas.

More About Daniel Newton Thorp:
Burial: 11 Mar 1965 in Friendship Cemetery, Hood County,
Texas Cause Of Death: Coronary Occlusion
Living In: 1910 Daniel and his family are living with his parents in Justice Precinct
1, Hood County, Texas
Living In: 1965 Haltom City, Texas
Occupation: Rancher

15. **SUSAN AVARILLA**^{3} **GARLAND** (Peter^2, Peter^1) was born on 20 Feb 1854 in Anderson County,
Texas. She died on 02 Aug 1920 in Granbury, Texas. She married David Lee Nutt, son of David
Nutt and Sarah Lee Landers on 28 Feb 1872 in Thorp Spring, Texas. He was born on 06 Jan
1848 in Neosha, Missouri. He died on 18 Feb 1929 in Granbury, Texas.

More About Susan Avarilla Garland:
Burial: 02 Aug 1920 in Granbury Cemetery, Granbury,
Texas Cause Of Death: Apoplexy

Notes for Susan Avarilla Garland:
Usually known as Sudie. Her death certificate gives her name as Mrs. Sudie Nutt.

More About David Lee Nutt:
Burial: 19 Feb 1929 in Granbury Cemetery, Granbury,
Texas
Cause Of Death: Cardiac Asthma
Living In: 1920 Granbury, Hood County, Texas
Occupation: 1880 in Granbury, Hood County, Texas; Grocer
Occupation: 1900 in Granbury, Hood County, Texas; Grocer
Occupation: 1910 in Granbury, Hood County, Texas; Retired

David Lee Nutt and Susan Avarilla Garland had the following children:

  i. MARTHA E.^{4} NUTT was born on 28 May 1874 in Granbury, Texas. She died on
    06 Jan 1951 in Los Angeles, California. She married (UNKNOWN) JONES.

    More About Martha E. Nutt:
    Burial: Forest Lawn Memorial Park, Glendale, Los Angeles County,
    California
    Living In: 1900 With her parents in Granbury, Texas.
    Occupation: 1900 - Book Keeper

    Notes for Martha E. Nutt:
    Has surname of Jones in 1900 U.S. census. California Death Index has her
    name as Martha Nutt.

  ii. SALLIE LUE NUTT was born on 29 Jan 1876 in Granbury, Texas. She died on 01
    Jan 1891 in Granbury, Texas.

48. iii. HENRY LEE NUTT was born on 01 Apr 1878 in Granbury, Texas. He died on 17 Aug 1956
    in Granbury, Texas. He married Euna Lee Barefoot, daughter of Lewis Barefoot and
    Mary Myrtle Oxier on 12 Aug 1903 in Chickasha, Oklahoma. She was born on 18 Feb
    1883 in Montague, Texas. She died on 10 Dec 1975 in Granbury,

Texas.

iv. JOE JAKE NUTT was born on 09 Feb 1884 in Granbury, Texas. He died on 01 Feb 1894 in Granbury, Texas.

Notes for Joe Jake Nutt:
Killed by a horse falling on him.

48. v. MARY SUE NUTT was born on 22 Jan 1898 in Granbury, Texas. She died on 28 Jun 1974 in Granbury, Texas. She married (1) LOUIS EDWARD FAULKNER, son of King Hiram Faulkner and Mary Elvira Crites on 08 Aug 1916 in Granbury, Texas. He was born on 24 Nov 1895 in Oklahoma. He died on 12 Nov 1964 in Houston, Texas. She married (2) FRANK WILLIAM MEHRTEN, son of John Mehrten and Palmar Clover on 12 Jan 1947. He was born on 23 Apr 1895 in Knox, Pennsylvania. He died on 30 Sep 1965 in Dallas, Texas.

16. **DANIEL N.**^{3} **GARLAND** (Peter^2, Peter^1) was born on 09 Apr 1864 in Thorp Spring, Hood County, Texas. He died on 28 Nov 1921 in Marlin, Texas. He married Inez Caldwell Toole, daughter of Alfred Toole and Belinda Yates on 18 Jan 1888 in Canadian, Choctaw Nation, Indian Territory (present day Canadian, Oklahoma). She was born on 26 May 1864 in Alabama. She died on 08 Apr 1931 in Dallas, Texas.

More About Daniel N. Garland:
Burial: 30 Nov 1921 in Rose Hill Cemetery, Chickasha, Oklahoma
Cause Of Death: Diabetic Coma
Living In: 1920 Daniel and Inez are living with their daughter, Ollie, in Houston Ward 4, Harris county, Texas
Occupation: 1900 in Chickasha, Chickashaw Nation, Indian Territory (present day Oklahoma); Stock Raiser
Occupation: 1910 in Chickasha ward 1, Grady County, Oklahoma; City Delivery of Dairy Milk

Notes for Daniel N. Garland:
Owner of Garland Dairy in Grady County, Oklahoma, 610 acres and 150 milk cows.
Moved to McAlester, Choctaw Nation, Indian Territory (present day McAlester, Oklahoma) in 1883.

More About Inez Caldwell Toole:
Burial: 10 Apr 1931 in Rose Hill Cemetery, Chickasha, Oklahoma
Cause Of Death: Cerebral Hemorrhage
Living In: 1930 Inez is living with her daughter, Ollie, in Dallas, Texas

Notes for Inez Caldwell Toole:
Member of the Choctaw Nation.

Daniel N. Garland and Inez Caldwell Toole had the following children:

i. OLLIE L.^{4} GARLAND was born on 21 Oct 1888 in Indian Territory (present day Oklahoma). She died on 15 Nov 1966 in Oklahoma. She married JOHN CHESTER BARR. He was born on 06 Oct 1888 in Kingston, Texas. He died on 03 Jul 1934 in Dallas, Texas.

More About Ollie L. Garland:

Burial: Rose Hill Cemetery, Chickasha, Oklahoma
Living In: 1966 in Chickasha, Oklahoma

    ii.   MILDRED GARLAND was born on 16 Nov 1892 in Indian Territory (present day Oklahoma). She died on 23 Oct 1901.

    More About Mildred Garland:
    Burial: Rose Hill Cemetery, Chickasha, Oklahoma

    iii.   ALLISON NELSON GARLAND was born on 01 Jul 1895 in Indian Territory (present day Oklahoma). He died on 10 Nov 1907.

    More About Allison Nelson Garland:
    Burial: Rose Hill Cemetery, Chickasha, Oklahoma

    iv.   MARY GARLAND was born on 27 Sep 1899 in Chickasha, Chickasha Nation, Indian Territory (present day Oklahoma). She died on 20 Dec 1951 in Houston, Texas. She married JAMES E. SMITH.

    More About Mary Garland:
    Burial: Rose Hill Cemetery, Chickasha, Oklahoma
    Living In: 1920 Living with her sister, Ollie, in Houston Ward 4, Harris County, Texas
    Living In: 1930 Living with her sister, Ollie, in Dallas, Texas

    v.   LOUISE GARLAND was born on 08 Aug 1903 in Indian Territory (present day Oklahoma). She died on 09 Jan 1919.

    More About Louise Garland:
    Burial: Rose Hill Cemetery, Chickasha, Oklahoma

17.   **SALINA J.**[3] **GARLAND** (Edward[2], Peter[1]) was born in Feb 1823 in Tennessee. She died in Dec 1903 in Denver, Colorado. She married Claudius Buchanan Hall, son of Thomas James Hall and Emma Wallace on 20 Nov 1845 in Maury County, Tennessee. He was born on 21 Jan 1820 in Tennessee. He died between 05 Sep 1870-07 Jun 1880.

More About Salina J. Garland:
Burial: 27 Dec 1903 in Fairmount Cemetery, Denver, Colorado
Living In: 1880 Lafayette, Christian County, Kentucky
Living In: Bet. 1885-1894 Nashville, Tennessee
Living In: 1900 Denver, Colorado

More About Claudius Buchanan Hall:
Living In: 1870 Lafayette, Kentucky
Occupation: 1850 in Christian County, Kentucky; Physician
Occupation: 1860 in Christian County, Kentucky; Physician
Occupation: 1870 in Lafayette, Christian County, Kentucky; Physician

Claudius Buchanan Hall and Salina J. Garland had the following children:

    i.   MARY ELLEN[4] HALL was born in Sep 1849 in Kentucky.

ii.   LIZZIE C. HALL was born in Nov 1859 in Kentucky.

More About Lizzie C. Hall:
Living In: 1880 Living with her mother in Lafayette, Christian County, Kentucky.
Living In: 1900   Living with her mother in Denver, Colorado.

49.   iii. ALLEN GARLAND HALL was born on 12 Jul 1862 in Kentucky. He died on 28 Nov 1915 in
               Nashville, Tennessee. He married Lillie Carter Gunn, daughter of Wesley Gunn and
               Martha Addie Grinter on 26 Feb 1885 in Kentucky. She was born on 02 Nov 1864 in
               Kentucky. She died on 08 Aug 1958 in Cadiz, Kentucky.

          iv.   CHARLIE HALL was born about 1865 in Kentucky.

18.   EDWARD WARREN[3] GARLAND (Edward[2], Peter[1]) was born on 28 Oct 1825 in Giles County,
      Tennessee. He died on 12 May 1897 in Texas. He married (1) JULIA REBECCA KIMBELL, daughter
      of John M. Kimbell and Sarah Angelina Elliott before 1878. She was born on 31 Mar 1845 in
      Republic of Texas. She died on 26 Jan 1908 in Texas. He married (2) MARY EMELINE JENKINS,
      daughter of James Wilson Jenkins and Sarah Dowd on 18 Jun 1845 in Tishomingo County,
      Mississippi. She was born on 25 Oct 1827 in Chatham County, North Carolina. She died on 21
      Feb 1887 in Hardin County, Tennessee.

      More About Edward Warren Garland:
      Burial: Garland Cemetery, Red River County, Texas
      Living In: 1845 With his uncle, Peter Garland, in Tishomingo County, Mississippi, two doors
      away from the home of Mary Emeline Jenkins
      Living In: Feb 1868 Red River County, Texas
      Occupation: 1850 in Tishomingo County, Mississippi; Merchant
      Occupation: 1880 in Precinct 7, Red River County, Texas; Farmer
      Military Service: Bet. 13 Sep 1847-10 Jul 1848 in Mexican War; Company C, Second
      Mississippi Infantry, U.S. Army
      Military Service: Civil War for C.S.A.
      Property: 1869 in Bowie County, Texas; 300 Acres
      Property: 1870 in Bowie County, Texas; 300 Acres
      Property: 1880 in Red River County, Texas; 36 Acres Improved and 50 Acres
      Unimproved
      Property: 1888 in Bowie County, Texas; 108 Acres and 8 city lots in DeKalb
      Property: 1889 in Bowie County, Texas; 108 Acres and 8 city lots in DeKalb
      Property: 1896 in Bowie County, Texas; 110 Acres and 7 city lots in DeKalb
      Property: 1897 in Bowie County, Texas; 110 Acres and 7 city lots in DeKalb

      Notes for Edward Warren Garland:
      Mustered in for Mexican War at Farmington, Mississippi. Mustered out in Vicksburg, Mississippi.

      November 25, 1869 Red River County, Texas voter registration shows Edward having lived in
      Red River County and Texas 22 months at that time.

      More About Julia Rebecca Kimbell:
      Burial: Garland Cemetery, Red River County, Texas
      Cause Of Death: Infection from a rat bite to her hand while reaching into a corn bin in her
      barn
      Living In: 1900 With her Garland children in Commissioner Precinct 3, Bowie County, Texas
      Occupation: 1860 in DeKalb, Texas; Seamstress
      Property: 1886 in Bowie County, Texas; 18 Acres

Edward Warren Garland and Julia Rebecca Kimbell had the following children:

50.　　i. JOSEPH EDWARD[4] GARLAND was born on 17 Mar 1878 in Red River County, Texas. He died on 01 Sep 1946 in Lamesa, Dawson County, Texas. He married Lou Ethel Bynum, daughter of Alfred Baker Bynum and Dorinda Sandal Baird on 21 May 1908 in Brownfield, Texas. She was born on 25 Apr 1890 in Whitewright, Grayson County, Texas. She died on 17 Sep 1969 in Lamesa, Dawson County, Texas.

51.　　ii. EMMA GEORGIE IRENE GARLAND was born on 23 Mar 1880 in Annona, Texas. She died on 17 Dec 1969 in Kerrville, Texas. She married LeRoy Ardis Edwards in May 1921 in Roscoe, Texas. He was born on 27 Feb 1881 in Sulphur Springs, Texas. He died on 05 Dec 1951 in Loraine, Texas.

　　　iii. RUFUS SMIZER MCKINNEY GARLAND was born on 03 Sep 1882 in Texas. He died on 07 Feb 1919 in North Atlantic Ocean (Returning from France after World War One).

　　　　More About Rufus Smizer McKinney Garland:
　　　　Burial: Loraine, Texas
　　　　Cause Of Death: Spanish Flu
　　　　Occupation: 1910 in Roscoe, Texas; Drug Store Prescriptionist
　　　　Occupation: 1917 in Loraine, Texas; Pharmacist
　　　　Military Service: 1918 in France; World War One (Medic)
　　　　Military Service: Spanish American War

　　　　Notes for Rufus Smizer McKinney Garland:
　　　　Died at sea on the way home from World War One military service in France due to the Great Flu Epidemic.
　　　　Never Married.

52.　　iv. MAGGIE AUGUSTA ESTELLE GARLAND was born in Aug 1884 in DeKalb, Texas. She died on 29 Jan 1955 in Sweetwater, Texas. She married Barna Haney, son of William Daniel Haney and Mamie H. Harkins on 24 May 1911 in Roscoe, Texas. He was born on 30 Nov 1887 in Temple, Bell County, Texas. He died on 27 Jan 1957 in Roscoe, Texas.

More About Mary Emeline Jenkins:
Burial: Roberts Cemetery, Conce, Hardin County, Tennessee
Cause Of Death: Consumption

More About Edward Warren Garland and Mary Emeline Jenkins:
Marriage Fact: 16 Jun 1845 in Date of Marriage Bond
Marriage Fact: Ceremony performed by J. C. Lowery, J.P.
Marriage Fact: Garland Family Oral History; Marriage lasted only one day.
Marriage Fact: Surety: G. L. Goff

19.　**RACHEL ANN**[3] **GARLAND** (Edward[2], Peter[1]) was born on 04 Oct 1844 in Henderson County, Tennessee. She died on 23 Aug 1929 in Franklin County, Alabama. She married Richard L. Winchester, son of Jonathan Winchester and Sarah Bruzil on 10 Feb 1867 in Pleasant Site, Franklin County, Alabama. He was born on 17 Feb 1839 in Heard County, Georgia. He died on 30 Jun 1919 in Pleasant Site, Franklin County, Alabama.

More About Rachel Ann Garland:
Burial: 24 Aug 1929 in Winchester Cemetery, Franklin County, Alabama

Living In: 1860 With her uncle, William Bullock, in Franklin County, Alabama

Notes for Rachel Ann Garland:
Headstone has first name spelled as Rachel.

More About Richard L. Winchester:
Burial: Winchester Cemetery, Franklin County, Alabama
Occupation: 1870 in Franklin County, Alabama; Farmer
Occupation: 1880 in Franklin County, Alabama; Farmer
Occupation: 1900 in Pleasant Site, Franklin County, Alabama; Farmer
Occupation: 1910 in Burleson, Franklin County, Alabama; Retired
Military Service: Bet. 06 Sep 1862-13 Apr 1863; Company I, 4th Alabama Cavalry, C.S.A.

Notes for Richard L. Winchester:
Enlisted on September 6, 1862 in Marshall County, Alabama and mustered in to 4th
Alabama Cavalry on September 22, 1862.
Discharged for disability from 4th Alabama Cavalry on April 13, 1863 at Chattanooga, Tennessee.

Richard L. Winchester and Rachel Ann Garland had the following children:

     i. MARY LILLIE[4] WINCHESTER was born on 12 Nov 1868 in Russellville, Alabama. She died on 29 Dec 1935 in Belmont, Tishomingo County, Mississippi.

    ii. JOHN J. WINCHESTER was born on 12 Jan 1869 in Franklin County, Alabama. He died on 20 Apr 1957 in Franklin County, Alabama.

    iii. EDWARD B. WINCHESTER was born on 03 Mar 1871 in Alabama. He died on 26 Apr 1940.

       More About Edward B. Winchester:
       Burial: Winchester Cemetery, Franklin County, Alabama

    iv. ALBERT C. WINCHESTER was born about 1874 in Alabama.

    v. HENRY J. WINCHESTER was born about 1878 in Alabama.

    vi. ALTA WINCHESTER was born in Jun 1882 in Alabama.

    vii. OCTAVUS G. WINCHESTER was born on 14 Oct 1885 in Alabama. He died on 20 Nov 1952.

       More About Octavus G. Winchester:
       Burial: Winchester Cemetery, Franklin County, Alabama

20. **MARTHA ANN**[3] **GARLAND** (Edward[2], Peter[1]) was born on 29 Sep 1849 in Mississippi. She died on 08 Jan 1877 in Tishomingo County, Mississippi. She married Francis Marion Winchester, son of Jonathan Winchester and Ellenor Glover in Oct 1869. He was born in Jun 1849 in Mississippi. He died after 28 Apr 1910 in Texas.

More About Martha Ann Garland:
Burial: Winchester Cemetery, Franklin County, Alabama

More About Francis Marion Winchester:
b: Abt. 1848
Occupation: 1870 in Tishomingo County, Mississippi; Farmer
Occupation: 1880 in Franklin County, Alabama; Farmer
Occupation: 1900 in Haskell County, Texas; Farmer
Occupation: 1910 in Weinert, Haskell County, Texas; Retired Farmer

Francis Marion Winchester and Martha Ann Garland had the following children:

      i.   CHARLES WALTER[4] WINCHESTER was born on 13 Mar 1876 in Alabama. He died on 21 Mar 1959 in Wellington, Collingsworth County, Texas.

          More About Charles Walter Winchester:
          Burial: Johnson Cemetery, Munday, Texas
          Occupation: Farmer

          Notes for Charles Walter Winchester:
          Birth date is from World War One draft registration.

      ii.   LEE WINCHESTER.

      iii.   CLARENCE WINCHESTER.

21.   MARTHA A. ELIZABETH[3] GARLAND (Thomas Lowery[2], Peter[1]) was born on 23 Nov 1829 in Madison County, Tennessee. She died on 07 May 1918 in Little Rock, Pulaski County, Arkansas. She married John Leemona Walsh, son of Johnathan Walsh and Winifred Kirby on 30 Nov 1856 in Madison County, Tennessee. He was born about 1825 in Tennessee. He died on 25 Mar 1885.

More About Martha A. Elizabeth Garland:
Living In: 1910 Living with her son, Walter, and his family in Little Rock, White County, Arkansas.

More About John Leemona Walsh:
Occupation: 1860 in District 4, Hardin County, Tennessee; Merchant
Occupation: 1870 in Liberty, White County, Arkansas; Farmer
Occupation: 1880 in Liberty, White County, Arkansas; Farmer

More About John Leemona Walsh and Martha A. Elizabeth Garland:
Marriage Fact: 18 Nov 1856 in Madison County, Tennessee; Marriage Licence Issued.

John Leemona Walsh and Martha A. Elizabeth Garland had the following children:

      i.   WILLIAM REDD[4] WALSH was born on 24 Jun 1858 in Tennessee. He died on 02 Apr 1859.

      ii.   IDA M. WALSH was born on 09 Nov 1859.

      iii.   IRA LEE WALSH was born on 26 Aug 1861. He died on 13 May 1934.

      iv.   WALTER GREEN WALSH was born on 18 Oct 1863. He died on 17 Nov 1936. He married NELLIE TILGMAN HURT. She was born about 1875.

          More About Walter Green Walsh:

Occupation: 1910 in Little Rock, White County, Arkansas; Rail Road Conductor

    v.   JOHN ROBERT WALSH was born on 22 Mar 1865. He died on 03 Feb 1867.

    vi.   JOSIE E. WALSH was born on 18 Oct 1866. She died on 21 Oct 1937. She married E. H. RIDLEY.

    vii.   EDGAR SIDNEY WALSH was born on 18 Aug 1869 in Arkansas. He married RHODA (UNKNOWN).

    More About Edgar Sidney Walsh:
Living In: 1910 Living with his brother, Walter, in Little Rock, White County, Arkansas.
Occupation: 1910 in Little Rock, White County, Arkansas; Telegrapher in Rail Road Office

    viii.   ORA E. WALSH was born on 18 Mar 1871. Ora E. died on 14 May 1871.

    ix.   ALBERTA WALSH was born on 12 Nov 1872. He died on 08 Dec 1900. He married S. R. HUDSON.

53.   x. MATTHEW LENORE WALSH was born on 08 Mar 1874 in Arkansas. He died on 04 Nov 1903 in Stamps, Arkansas. He married Mabel May Lowe, daughter of Millard Lowe and Julia Knowlen on 17 Nov 1900 in Corning, Arkansas.

22.   **WILLIAM WIRT**[3] **GARLAND** (Thomas Lowery[2], Peter[1]) was born on 03 Jan 1835 in Madison County, Tennessee. He died in 1908 in Conway County, Arkansas. He married Mary Elizabeth McKnight on 19 Dec 1854 in Madison County, Tennessee. She was born in Aug 1836 in Tennessee. She died in 1914 in Conway County, Arkansas.

More About William Wirt Garland:
Burial: Elmwood Cemetery, Morrilton, Conway County, Arkansas
Occupation: 1850 in Madison County, Tennessee; Farmer
Occupation: 1860 in Liberty, White County, Arkansas; Farmer
Occupation: 1870 in Augusta, Arkansas; Life Insurance Agent
Occupation: Bet. 1880-1898; Merchant (Grocery store) in Morrillton, Arkansas.
Occupation: 03 Jun 1880 in Augusta, Woodruff County, Arkansas; no occupation given on 1880 U.S. census
Occupation: 12 Jun 1900 in Morrilton, Conway County, Arkansas; no occupation listed on 1900 U.S. census
Occupation: Mayor of Augusta, Arkansas.
Occupation: Deputy Sheriff of Woodruff County, Arkansas.
Occupation: Constable in Augusta, Arkansas
Military Service: Company H, 36th Arkansas Infantry, C.S.A.

Notes for William Wirt Garland:
Marriage Bond issued December 18, 1854, Married December 19, 1854.

Enlisted in Company H, 36th Arkansas Infantry June 16, 1862 at Green Springs, Arkansas and was elected 3rd Lieutenant, later made Brevet 2nd Lieutenant. Mustered into service on June 25, 1862

in Springfield, Arkansas. Wounded at battle of Helena, Arkansas on July 4, 1863.

William and his wife adopted Ora before June 3, 1880

More About Mary Elizabeth McKnight:
Burial: Elmwood Cemetery, Morrilton, Conway County, Arkansas

William Wirt Garland and Mary Elizabeth McKnight had the following child:

    i. ORA[4] GARLAND was born on 04 Jun 1873 in Arkansas. She died on 16 Jun 1940 in Conway County, Arkansas. She married TAYLOR AYLETTE DOWDLE. He was born on 10 Sep 1869. He died on 04 Nov 1930.

        More About Ora Garland:
        Burial: Elmwood Cemetery, Morrilton, Conway County, Arkansas

23.   **ROBERT REAMEY[3] GARLAND** (Thomas Lowery[2], Peter[1]) was born on 07 Jan 1841 in Madison County, Tennessee. He died on 08 Oct 1923 in Emmet, Nevada County, Arkansas. He married Hannah Josephine McSwain on 10 Sep 1865 in Columbia County, Arkansas. She was born on 30 Aug 1848 in Marshall County, Mississippi. She died on 16 Jun 1915 in Emmet, Nevada County, Arkansas.

More About Robert Reamey Garland:
Burial: Snell Cemetery, Emmet, Nevada County, Arkansas
Living In: 1860 Living with his sister, Martha, and her family in District 4, Hardin County, Tennessee.
Occupation: 1870 in Alabama, Columbia County, Arkansas;
Farmer
Occupation: 1880 in Hadley, Columbia County, Arkansas; Farmer
Occupation: 1900 in Emmet, Nevada County, Arkansas; Farmer
Occupation: 1910 in Emmet, Nevada County, Arkansas; Farmer
Occupation: 1920 in Emmet, Nevada County, Arkansas; Farmer
Military Service: Company E, 1st Battalion Arkansas Cavalry, C.S.A.

More About Hannah Josephine McSwain:
Burial: Snell Cemetery, Emmet, Nevada County, Arkansas

Robert Reamey Garland and Hannah Josephine McSwain had the following children:

    i.   MARTHA E.[4] GARLAND was born about 1867 in Arkansas.

    ii.   OCTAVIA M. GARLAND was born about 1869 in Arkansas.

    iii. EZEKIAL GARLAND was born about 1872 in Arkansas.

    iv. MARY E. GARLAND was born about 1874 in Arkansas.

    v.   JOHN M. GARLAND was born in Jul 1876 in Arkansas.

    vi. THOMAS LUCIUS GARLAND was born in Aug 1878 in Arkansas. He died in 1953.

    vii. ALICE JOSEPHINE GARLAND was born in Jul 1881 in Arkansas. She died in 1954.

    viii. DOUGLAS GARLAND was born in Nov 1884 in Arkansas.

    ix.   WARREN W. GARLAND was born in Aug 1889 in Arkansas.

24.   JOSEPH DANIEL[3] GARLAND (Thomas Lowery[2], Peter[1]) was born on 21 Apr 1843 in Madison County, Tennessee. He died on 05 Jan 1918 in Polk County, Arkansas. He married Zuritha Ann Parrish on 9 Aug 1866 in Grand Glaze, Jackson County, Arkansas. She was born on 01 Jan 1843 in Tipton County, Tennessee. She died in Jan 1927.

More About Joseph Daniel Garland:
Burial: 07 Jan 1918 in Owens Chapel Cemetery, Acorn, Polk County, Arkansas
Living In: 1860 Living with his sister, Martha, and her family in District 4, Hardin County, Tennessee.
Occupation: 1866 in Grand Glaze, Jackson County, Arkansas; Shoe and Boot maker.
Occupation: 1880 in Hadley, Columbia County, Arkansas; Farmer
Occupation: 1883 in near Acorn, Polk County, Arkansas; Farmer
Occupation: 1900 in Eagle Gap, Polk County, Arkansas; Farmer
Occupation: 1910 in Eagle Gap, Polk County, Arkansas; Farmer
Occupation: Acorn, Arkansas; Justice of the Peace
Occupation: Director of Acorn, Arkansas school district
Occupation: Polk County, Arkansas; County and Probate Judge
Occupation: Columbia County, Arkansas; Justice of the Peace
Military Service: Bet. 22 Feb 1862-04 Jul 1865; Company A, 36th Arkansas Infantry, C.S.A.

Notes for Joseph Daniel Garland:
Military Engagements: Prarie Grove, Helena, Pleasant Hill, and Jenkins Ferry. Enlisted at Searcy, Arkansas
Paroled on July 4, 1865.
Made Ensign of 36th Arkansas Infantry on March 14, 1863
Promoted from Third Sergeant to First Lieutenant on August 8, 1864 with a date of rank of August 3, 1864.

Newspaper Jan 10,1918

Well Known Polk County Passes To Beyond -
Judge J. D. Garland of Acorn Departed This Life Saturday Night. A leader in Community.

Judge J. D. Garland, one of the pioneer residents of the Acorn community departed this life at 8 o'clock Saturday night at the home of his son, J.C. Garland, at Walter Valley farm. Judge Garland, though advanced in years, had been in uncommonly good health this fall and winter, and even during the day of his death he had in good spirits, the end coming to him almost without warning, being taken with severe pain in the chest just as the family gathered at this supper table and passed away shortly after that.

The funeral services were held Monday afternoon at 1 o'clock at the Owens Chapel cemetery, the services being in charge of the Rev. J.V. Kelley of the M. E. Church, South.

Mr. Garland served with honor in the Confederate Army during the last three years of the war. Mr. and Mrs. Garland came to Polk County about 34 years ago, locating on the place now known as the Walter Valley farm, and continuing to reside there throughout their days. Mr. Garland was not only a pioneer settler of the Acorn community, but was a pioneer in every movement that had for its aim and object the moral, social, spiritual and intellectual uplift of the community. He was the first teacher of the Acorn School, a leader in the neighborhood singings and prayer meetings, the school and the movement for the improvement of agricultural conditions and served one term as county judge.

He was director of the Acorn school district, and had served his township as Justice of the Peace, but even long after he gave up active life along these lines, his influence was a great factor in the development of the community.

He was Acorn correspondent for The Star for a long time, using the pseudonym, " American" Hi item always breathed the spirit of optimism and progress, and thru them he was more helpful than he knew to many readers of The Star.

More About Zuritha Ann Parrish:
Burial: Owens Chapel Cemetery, Acorn, Polk County, Arkansas

More About Joseph Daniel Garland and Zuritha Ann Parrish:
Marriage Fact: ; Married by Rev. John Cook, Methodist Minister

Joseph Daniel Garland and Zuritha Ann Parrish had the following children:

      i.   ENOS LOWERY[4] GARLAND was born on 21 Mar 1868 in White County, Arkansas. He died in 1871.

         More About Enos Lowery Garland:
         Burial: Carter Graveyard, near Russell, Arkansas

54.   ii. BONNIE EARL GARLAND was born on 29 Nov 1871 in near Bradford, White County, Arkansas. She died on 11 Aug 1959 in Higo, Choctaw County, Oklahoma. She married Thomas Wright on 05 Feb 1888 in Polk County, Arkansas. He was born about 1860 in Tennessee.

      iii. JOVIAN CRAWLEY GARLAND was born on 25 Mar 1873 in White County, Arkansas. He died in Feb 1971. He married Blanche Sogle on 03 Apr 1898 in Polk County, Arkansas. She was born in 1880. She died in 1965.

         More About Jovian Crawley Garland:
         Burial: Owens Chapel Cemetery, Acorn, Polk County, Arkansas

      iv. BERTHA HEARN GARLAND was born on 28 Oct 1877 in Columbia County, Arkansas.

25.   JAMES MARTIN[3] SIMMONS (Harriet Wilmot[2] Garland, Peter[1] Garland) was born on 05 Dec 1830 in Madison County, Tennessee. He died on 26 Nov 1912 in Henderson County, Tennessee. He married (1) **MARY ELIZABETH CHESSIER** on 18 Mar 1856. She was born on 11 Mar 1836 in Halifax, Virginia. She died on 01 Aug 1896 in Henderson County, Tennessee. He married (2) **ANNA H. (UNKNOWN)** about 1897. She was born in Feb 1862 in Mississippi.

More About James Martin Simmons:
Burial: Old Pisgah Cemetery, Chester County, Tennessee
Occupation: 1880 in District 1, Madison County, Tennessee; Farmer
Occupation: 1900 in Civil District 6, Chester County, Tennessee; Farmer
Occupation: 1910 in Henderson, Chester County, Tennessee; Farmer

More About Mary Elizabeth Chessier:
Burial: Old Pisgah Cemetery, Chester County, Tennessee

James Martin Simmons and Mary Elizabeth Chessier had the following

    children: i. HIRAM B.[4] SIMMONS was born about 1860 in Tennessee.

    ii.   ELIZABETH SIMMONS was born on 05 Nov 1861 in Tennessee. She died on 22 May 1940.

More About Elizabeth Simmons:
Burial: Old Pisgah Cemetery, Chester County, Tennessee

    iii.   ALCOMA SIMMONS was born about 1867 in Tennessee.

    iv.   DANIEL SIMMONS was born about 1872 in Tennessee.

    v.   MINNIE M. SIMMONS was born in Oct 1875 in Tennessee.

26.   PETER GARLAND[3] SIMMONS (Harriet Wilmot[2] Garland, Peter[1] Garland) was born on 15 Oct 1832 in Madison County, Tennessee. He died before 11 Jul 1915. He married Anna Elizabeth Chesser, daughter of William Chesser and Lon Muse on 10 Sep 1857 in Madison County, Tennessee. She was born on 11 Mar 1837 in Virginia. She died on 11 Jul 1915 in Henderson, Chester County, Tennessee.

More About Peter Garland Simmons:
Living In: 1860 Peter and his family are living with his mother in law in District 1 Madison County, Tennessee
Occupation: 1850 in Madison County, Tennessee; Farmer
Occupation: 1860 in District 1, Madison County, Tennessee; Farmer

More About Anna Elizabeth Chesser:
Burial: 12 Jul 1915 in Old Pisgah Cemetery, Chester County, Tennessee

Peter Garland Simmons and Anna Elizabeth Chesser had the following children:

    i.   MARY[4] SIMMONS was born about 1858 in Tennessee.

    ii.   JOHN SIMMONS was born about Dec 1859 in Tennessee.

27.   MARTHA JANE[3] SIMMONS (Harriet Wilmot[2] Garland, Peter[1] Garland) was born on 16 Nov 1833 in Madison County, Tennessee. She died on 25 Apr 1890. She married (1) **JOHN W. BROWDER** on 05 Sep 1853 in Madison County, Tennessee. He was born on 12 Sep 1824 in Virginia. He died after 13 Sep 1866. She married **JOSEPH A. DAVIS**. He was born on 29 Apr 1830 in Virginia. He died on 18 Oct 1902.

More About Martha Jane Simmons:
Burial: Old Pisgah Cemetery, Chester County, Tennessee

More About John W. Browder:
Burial: Old Pisgah Cemetery, Chester County, Tennessee
Occupation: 1860 in District 1, Madison County, Tennessee; Farmer

John W. Browder and Martha Jane Simmons had the following children:

    i.   JOSEPH[4] BROWDER was born about 1855 in Tennessee.

    ii.   MALVINA BROWDER was born about Dec 1859 in Tennessee.

More About Malvina Browder:
Living In: 1880 Living with her mother and step father in District 1, Madison County, Tennessee.

More About Joseph A. Davis:
Burial: Old Pisgah Cemetery, Chester County, Tennessee
Occupation: 1880 in District 1, Madison County, Tennessee; Farmer

28.   **MARY FRANCES**[3] **SIMMONS** (Harriet Wilmot[2] Garland, Peter[1] Garland) was born on 15 Apr 1839 in Madison County, Tennessee. She died on 16 May 1921 in Henderson, Chester County, Tennessee. She married Edward L. Sanford on 23 Dec 1857 in Madison County, Tennessee. He was born about 1837 in Tennessee. He died in 1897.

More About Mary Frances Simmons:
Burial: 18 May 1921 in Sanford Rodgers Cemetery, Chester County, Tennesee
Living In: 1920 Living with her son, James, in Civil District 6, Chester County, Tennessee.
Occupation: 1900 in Civil District 6, Chester County, Tennessee; Farmer
Occupation: 1910 in Civil District 6, Chester County, Tennessee

Notes for Mary Frances Simmons:
1900 U.S. census gives birth month and year as April 1839.

More About Edward L. Sanford:
Burial: Sanford Rodgers Cemetery, Chester County, Tennessee
Occupation: 1860 in District 1, Madison County, Tennessee; Farmer
Occupation: 1880 in District 1, Madison County, Tennessee; Farmer

Edward L. Sanford and Mary Frances Simmons had the following children:

    i.   JOHN W.[4] SANFORD was born in Aug 1861 in Tennessee.

        More About John W. Sanford:
        Living In: 1900 Living with his mother in Civil District 6, Chester County, Tennessee.
        Living In: 1910 Living with his mother in Civil District 6, Chester County, Tennessee.
        Living In: 1920 Living with his brother, James, in Civil District 6, Chester County, Tennessee.
        Occupation: 1900 in Civil District 6, Chester County, Tennessee; Farm Manager on his mother's farm

    ii.   JAMES E. SANFORD was born in Aug 1866 in Tennessee.

        More About James E. Sanford:
        Living In: 1900 Living with his mother in Civil District 6, Chester County, Tennessee.
        Living In: 1910 Living with his mother in Civil District 6, Chester County, Tennessee.
        Occupation: 1900 in Civil District 6, Chester County, Tennessee; Farmer on his mother's farm.
        Occupation: 1910 in Civil District 6, Chester County, Tennessee; Farmer on his mother's farm.
        Occupation: 1920 in Civil District 6, Chester County, Tennessee; Farmer

    iii.   LUCY W. SANFORD was born in Dec 1869 in Tennessee.

More About Lucy W. Sanford:
Living In: 1900 Living with her mother in Civil District 6, Chester County, Tennessee.
Living In: 1910 Living with her mother in Civil District 6, Chester County, Tennessee.
Living In: 1920 Living with her brother, James, in Civil District 6, Chester County, Tennessee.

29.   **JOHN CRAWLEY**[3] **SIMMONS** (Harriet Wilmot[2] Garland, Peter[1] Garland) was born on 03 Jan 1841 in Madison County, Tennessee. He died on 10 Feb 1911 in Henderson, Chester County, Tennessee. He married Rebecca L. Garland, daughter of William Wirt Garland and Elizabeth A. Exum on 22 Oct 1867 in Madison County, Tennessee. She was born on 28 Oct 1847 in Chester County, Tennessee. She died on 07 Apr 1921 in Civil District 6, Chester County, Tennessee.

More About John Crawley Simmons:
Cause Of Death: Pneumonia
Living In: 1860 Living with his brother, Peter, in the household of Peter's mother in law in Madison County, Tennessee.
Living In: 1900 Living with his sister, Mary, and her family in Chester County, Tennessee.
Living In: 1910 Living as a boarder with Mrs. Frances E. Ball in Chester County, Tennessee.
Occupation: 1870 in District 1, Madison County, Tennessee; Farmer
Occupation: 1880 in District 1, Madison County, Tennessee; Farmer
Occupation: 1900 in Civil district 6, Chester County, Tennessee; Day Laborer
Occupation: 1910 in Chester County, Tennessee; Farm Laborer

Notes for John Crawley Simmons:
1900 U. S. census has month and year of birth as May 1841.
Listed as divorced on 1900 U.S. census and as widowed on 1910 U.S. census.

More About Rebecca L. Garland:
Burial: 09 Apr 1921 in Chester County, Tennessee
Cause Of Death: Cerebral Embolism
Living In: 1910 Henderson, Chester County, Tennessee
Living In: 1920 Henderson, Chester County, Tennessee
Occupation: 1900 in Civil District 6, Chester County, Tennessee; Farmer

Notes for Rebecca L. Garland:
Listed as divorced in 1900 and 1910 U.S. census. Listed as a widow in 1920 U.S. census.

More About John Crawley Simmons and Rebecca L. Garland:
Marriage License: 22 Oct 1867 in Madison County, Tennessee
Marriage Fact: ; Married by E. L. Fisher, L.D., Memphis Conference

John Crawley Simmons and Rebecca L. Garland had the following children:
    i.   UDA W.[4] SIMMONS was born about 1869 in Tennessee.

    ii.   ADA K. SIMMONS was born in Nov 1875 in Tennessee.

More About Ada K. Simmons:
Living In: 1900 Living with her mother in Civil District 6, Chester County, Tennessee.
Living In: 1910 Living with her mother in Henderson, Chester County, Tennessee.
Living In: 1920 Living with her mother in Henderson, Chester County, Tennessee.

30. **NANCY WILMOT[3] SIMMONS** (Harriet Wilmot[2] Garland, Peter[1] Garland) was born on 03 Jan 1843 in Madison County, Tennessee. She died on 09 Feb 1894 in Annona, Texas. She married Thomas Crutcher Holt on 02 Feb 1862 in Holly Springs, Mississippi. He was born on 01 May 1833 in Tennessee. He died on 11 Nov 1909 in Annona, Texas.

More About Nancy Wilmot Simmons:
Burial: Garland Cemetery, Red River County, Texas
Living In: 1860 Living with her sister, Martha, and her family in District 1, Madison County, Tennessee.

More About Thomas Crutcher Holt:
Burial: Garland Cemetery, Red River County, Texas
Occupation: 1870 in Township 6, Range 15, Franklin County, Alabama; Carpenter
Occupation: 1880 in Precinct 6, Red River County, Texas; Farmer

Thomas Crutcher Holt and Nancy Wilmot Simmons had the following children:

    i.   ANDREW BELL[4] HOLT was born on 25 Dec 1862 in Mississippi. He died on 03 Oct 1897 in San Angelo, Texas. He married EMMA FERGUSON.

    ii.   THOMAS CRAWLEY HOLT was born on 30 Jun 1864 in Mississippi. He died on 08 Apr 1865.

    iii.   HARRIET ELIZABETH HOLT was born in 1866 in Tennessee. She died in 1875 in Bowie County, Texas.

    iv.   EDGAR EUGENE HOLT was born on 29 Feb 1868 in Henderson Station, Tennessee. He died on 14 Feb 1964 in Ardmore, Oklahoma. He married Rosetta Snell on 01 May 1888 in Annona, Texas. She was born on 11 Jul 1873. She died on 09 Jul 1954 in Greeneville, Oklahoma.

    v.   PETER GARLAND HOLT was born on 30 Apr 1870 in Tennessee. He died on 25 May 1934 in Corsicana, , Texas. He married Alie May Pillon on 04 Sep 1901.

        More About Peter Garland Holt:
        Burial: 26 May 1934 in Oakwood Cemetery, Corsicana, Texas

    vi.   JESSIE ESTELLE HOLT was born on 27 Jun 1873 in Alabama. She died on 29 Aug 1966 in Scurry County, Texas. She married (1) WILLIAM OSCAR PRESTON on 16 Jun 1889. She married TOM PRUITT.

    vii.   ROSALINE MAY HOLT was born on 18 Mar 1875 in Texas. She died in 1900. She married Charlie Griffen on 30 Oct 1898.

    viii.   TOMMIE LENA HOLT was born on 03 Jan 1878 in Red River County, Texas. She died on 01 Sep 1917 in Texas. She married George Francis Warthan on 16 Jan 1896.

    ix.   HAL OLIVER HOLT was born on 23 Jul 1880 in Red River County, Texas. He died on

07 Nov 1968 in Lubbock, Texas. He married Cynthia Elizabeth Pillon, daughter of John Crockett Pillon and Josephine Lindley on 15 Dec 1906. She was born on 20 Feb 1889 in Texas. She died on 10 Jan 1972 in Lamesa, Texas.

More About Hal Oliver Holt:
Burial: 10 Nov 1968 in Lamesa Memorial Park, Lamesa, Texas
Cause Of Death: Renal Failure
Living In: 1968 Lamesa, Texas
Occupation: Farmer

x. MARTHA LOUISA FRANCES HOLT was born on 21 Oct 1882 in Texas. She died on 07 Feb 1971 in Lamesa, Texas. She married Milton Oscar Grant on 18 Dec 1898.

31. MARGARET C.[3] GARLAND (John Calhoun[2], Peter[1]) was born on 13 Apr 1838 in Madison County, Tennessee. She died on 23 Dec 1911 in Annona, Texas. She married Nimrod B. Winston on 17 Sep 1856 in Madison County, Tennessee. He was born on 04 Jan 1836 in Tennessee. He died on 29 Jul 1903 in Annona, Texas.

More About Margaret C. Garland:
Burial: Garland Cemetery, Red River County, Texas

More About Nimrod B. Winston:
Burial: Garland Cemetery, Red River County, Texas
Occupation: 1860 in Bowie County, Texas; Farmer
Occupation: 1870 in Red River County, Texas; Merchant
Occupation: 1880 in Red River County, Texas; Farmer

Nimrod B. Winston and Margaret C. Garland had the following children:

i. JOHN G.[4] WINSTON was born on 15 Jul 1868 in Texas. He died on 19 Dec 1896.

More About John G. Winston:
Burial: Garland Cemetery, Red River County, Texas

55. ii. LILLIE THOMAS WINSTON was born on 08 Dec 1858 in Bowe County, Texas. She died on 04 Aug 1938 in Red River County, Texas. She married THOMAS JEFFERSON LAWSON. He was born on 27 Feb 1849 in Texas. He died on 06 Apr 1887 in Texas.

32. JOSEPH DANIEL RAMEY[3] GARLAND (John Calhoun[2], Peter[1]) was born on 23 Jun 1840 in Montgomery, Tennessee. He died on 21 Apr 1914 in Annona, Texas. He married (1) **JESSIE S. LATIMER**, daughter of Henry Russell Latimer and Lucinda Lou Shelton on 27 Oct 1873 in Red River County, Texas. She was born on 06 Feb 1853 in Texas. She died on 06 Jul 1895 in Annona, Texas. He married (2) **AVIS IDELLA AGNES SHELTON**, daughter of Eli Jenway Shelton and Martha Ann Elizabeth Yates on 23 Nov 1897 in Lamar County, Texas. She was born on 12 Jan 1857 in Lamar County, Texas. She died on 22 Nov 1935 in Nacogdoches, Texas.

More About Joseph Daniel Ramey Garland:
Burial: Garland Cemetery, Red River County, Texas
Living In: 1870 Living with his parents in Precinct 3, Red River county, Texas.
Occupation: 1880 in Precinct 8, Red River County, Texas; Farmer
Occupation: 1900 in Justice Precinct 8, Red River County, Texas; Farmer
Occupation: 1910 in Justice Precinct 8, Red River County, Texas; Farmer
Military Service: 04 Mar 1862; Enlisted in Company G, 34th Regiment, Texas Cavalry, C.S.A.

Property: 1880 in Red River County, Texas; 500 Acres Improved and 2500 Acres Unimproved

Notes for Joseph Daniel Ramey Garland:
Promoted to Sgt. Major on January 15, 1864.

Captured by troops of Brig. General Joseph A. Mower near Yellow Bayou, Louisiana on May 18, 1864.

Held as a Prisoner of War in New Orleans, Louisiana until July 22, 1864 when he was exchanged at Red River Landing.

-

In St. Lois, U.S.A. General Hospital, New Orleans, Louisiana from July 11, 1864 until July 21, 1864 for intermittent fever.

More About Jessie S. Latimer:
Burial: Garland Cemetery, Red River County, Texas

Notes for Jessie S. Latimer:
Birth name might be Susan Jesse Latimer.

Joseph Daniel Ramey Garland and Jessie S. Latimer had the following children:

      i. JACK R.[4] GARLAND was born on 06 Sep 1875 in Annona, Texas. He died on 27 Aug 1956 in Wichita Falls, Texas.

          More About Jack R. Garland:
          Burial: 29 Aug 1956 in Grove Hill Cemetery, Dallas, Texas
          Cause Of Death: Coronary Occlusion
          Occupation: Merchant

      ii. NANCY LUCINDA GARLAND was born in 1876 in Texas. She died in 1955.

56.   iii. JOELLA G. GARLAND was born on 02 Apr 1878 in Annona, Texas. She died on 22 Mar 1946 in Clarkesville, Texas. She married (1) JOHN R. PEEK on 18 Feb 1903 in Red River County, Texas. He was born on 09 Oct 1877. He died on 08 Nov 1909. She married JOHN HIRAM DOOLEY. He was born on 24 Jul 1870 in Lamar County, Texas. He died on 28 May 1951 in Sherman, Texas.

57.   iv. MARY LEDA GARLAND was born on 20 Jan 1880 in Annona, Texas. She died on 18 Oct 1967 in Sherman, Texas. She married JOSEPH B. WRIGHT. He was born on 19 Dec 1887 in Grenada, Mississippi. He died on 21 Jan 1967 in Sherman, Texas.

58.   v. WIRT ROBERT GARLAND was born on 31 Mar 1881 in Annona, Texas. He died on 18 May 1963 in Texarkana, Texas. He married Lola Prudence Dellinger, daughter of Charles F. Dellinger and Sarah Eaker in 1902 in Annona, Texas. She was born on 03 Aug 1881 in Annona, Texas. She died on 19 Feb 1969 in Clarkesville, Texas.

      vi. JOSEPH D. GARLAND was born on 21 May 1888 in Annona, Texas. He died on 08 Nov 1888.

          More About Joseph D. Garland:

Burial: Garland Cemetery, Red River County, Texas

Notes for Joseph D. Garland:
Cemetery transcription gives May 21, 1888 as birth date.

59.   vii. ROY LATIMER GARLAND was born on 05 Apr 1892 in Annona, Texas. He died on 01 May
                1968 in Texarkana, Bowie County, Texas. He married Mamie Claire Pipkin, daughter
                of Thomas P. Pipkin and Mollie Gaines in Kaufman, Texas. She was born on 19 Mar
                1891. She died on 07 Nov 1957 in Clarkesville, Texas.

More About Avis Idella Agnes Shelton:
Burial: 23 Nov 1935 in Pleasant Hill Cemetery, Paris, Lamar County, Texas
Living In: 1920 San Marcos, Hays County, Texas

Notes for Avis Idella Agnes Shelton:
Usually known as Idella or Della. Headstone has Della S. Garland.

33.   RUTH[3] GARLAND (John Calhoun[2], Peter[1]). She married **JAMES GARLAND**. He was born about 1800.

James Garland and Ruth Garland had the following children:
60.   i. JAMES POLK[4] GARLAND was born about 1848. He married J. (UNKNOWN). She was born
                about 1858.

           ii.   LAURA GARLAND. She married ROBERT SHAVERS.

34.   **REBECCA L.**[3] **GARLAND** (William Wirt[2], Peter[1]) was born on 28 Oct 1847 in Chester County,
       Tennessee. She died on 07 Apr 1921 in Civil District 6, Chester County, Tennessee. She
       married John Crawley Simmons, son of James Martin Simmons and Harriet Wilmot Garland on
       22 Oct 1867 in Madison County, Tennessee. He was born on 03 Jan 1841 in Madison County,
       Tennessee. He died on 10 Feb 1911 in Henderson, Chester County, Tennessee.

More About Rebecca L. Garland:
Burial: 09 Apr 1921 in Chester County, Tennessee
Cause Of Death: Cerebral Embolism
Living In: 1910 Henderson, Chester County, Tennessee
Living In: 1920 Henderson, Chester County, Tennessee
Occupation: 1900 in Civil District 6, Chester County, Tennessee; Farmer

Notes for Rebecca L. Garland:
Listed as divorced in 1900 and 1910 U.S. census. Listed as a widow in 1920 U.S. census.

More About John Crawley Simmons:
Cause Of Death: Pneumonia
Living In: 1860 Living with his brother, Peter, in the household of Peter's mother in law in
Madison County, Tennessee.
Living In: 1900 Living with his sister, Mary, and her family in Chester County, Tennessee.
Living In: 1910 Living as a boarder with Mrs. Frances E. Ball in Chester County, Tennessee.
Occupation: 1870 in District 1, Madison County, Tennessee; Farmer
Occupation: 1880 in District 1, Madison County, Tennessee; Farmer
Occupation: 1900 in Civil district 6, Chester County, Tennessee; Day
Laborer
Occupation: 1910 in Chester County, Tennessee; Farm Laborer

Notes for John Crawley Simmons:
1900 U. S. census has month and year of birth as May 1841.
Listed as divorced on 1900 U.S. census and as widowed on 1910 U.S. census.

More About John Crawley Simmons and Rebecca L. Garland:
Marriage License: 22 Oct 1867 in Madison County, Tennessee
Marriage Fact: Married by E. L. Fisher, L.D., Memphis Conference

John Crawley Simmons and Rebecca L. Garland had the following children:

     i.   UDA W.[4] SIMMONS was born about 1869 in Tennessee.

     ii.   ADA K. SIMMONS was born in Nov 1875 in Tennessee.

        More About Ada K. Simmons:
        Living In: 1900 Living with her mother in Civil District 6, Chester County, Tennessee.
        Living In: 1910 Living with her mother in Henderson, Chester County, Tennessee.
        Living In: 1920 Living with her mother in Henderson, Chester County, Tennessee.

35.   FELIX EXUM[3] GARLAND (William Wirt[2], Peter[1]) was born in Apr 1854 in Chester County, Tennessee. He died on 29 Mar 1912 in Henderson county, Tennessee. He married Nannie Deaton, daughter of John Deaton and Jane Clemmons about 1908. She was born in May 1877 in Tennessee.

More About Felix Exum Garland:
Burial: Garland Cemetery, Henderson, Tennessee
Living In: 1880 With his father in Madison County, Tennessee
Living In: 1900 With his father in Chester County, Tennessee
Occupation: 1870 in Madison County, Tennessee; Farm Hand on his father's farm
Occupation: 1880 in Madison County, Tennessee; Farmer
Occupation: 1900 in Chester County, Tennessee; Farmer
Occupation: 1910 in Civil district 6, Chester County, Tennessee; Farmer

Felix Exum Garland and Nannie Deaton had the following child:

     i.   WILLIAM WIRT[4] GARLAND.

Generation 4

36.   COLUMBUS ERASTUS[4] THORNTON (Mary Anna[3] Garland, Peter[2] Garland, Peter[1] Garland) was born on 23 Dec 1855 in Anderson County, Texas. He died on 20 Apr 1937 in Spur, Texas. He married MARY J. CRAWFORD. She was born about 1857 in Arkansas.

More About Columbus Erastus Thornton:
Burial: 21 Apr 1937 in Dickens Cemetery, Dickens, Dickens County, Texas
Occupation: 1880 in Precinct 7, Erath County, Texas; Farmer

Columbus Erastus Thornton and Mary J. Crawford had the following children:

     i.   ANNA[5] THORNTON. She married OSGOOD PIERCE CLARK.

     ii.   ERAL THORNTON. He married LAURA A. (UNKNOWN).

    iii.   FELIX R. THORNTON was born about 1878 in Texas.

    iv.   GWEN THORNTON.

    v.   IDA THORNTON.

    vi.   JOE THORNTON.

    vii.   LAWRENCE THORNTON.

    viii.   LUTHER M. THORNTON was born on 15 Jul 1879 in Erath County, Texas. He died on 05 Dec 1945 in Matador, Motley County, Texas.

        More About Luther M. Thornton:
        Burial: Red Mud Cemetery, Spur, Dickens County, Texas

    ix.   RUBY THORNTON.

37.   **THOMAS PETER**[4] **THORNTON** (Mary Anna[3] Garland, Peter[2] Garland, Peter[1] Garland) was born on 27 May 1857 in Dripping Springs, Texas. He died on 29 Jan 1917 in Stephenville, Erath County, Texas. He married **PARCINDA GORDON**. She was born on 06 Apr 1861 in Tyler, Texas. She died on 22 May 1941 in Erath County, Texas.

More About Thomas Peter Thornton:
Burial: 30 Jan 1917 in Hannibal Cemetery, Hannibal, Erath County, Texas
Occupation: Farmer

Notes for Thomas Peter Thornton:
Headstone has May 27, 1858 for date of birth. Death certificate has May 27, 1857 for date of birth.

More About Parcinda Gordon:
Burial: 23 May 1941 in Hannibal Cemetery, Hannibal, Erath County, Texas

Thomas Peter Thornton and Parcinda Gordon had the following children:

    i.   ANNA GERTRUDE[5] THORNTON. She married CHESTER SMITH. She married MARTIN FULFER.

    ii.   HELEN THORNTON. She married Naith McInroe on 15 Feb 1910.

    iii.   ANNA MAUDE THORNTON was born on 18 Aug 1878. She married STEPHEN A. MOONEY.

    iv.   WESLEY THORNTON was born on 17 Mar 1884. He died on 11 Jun 1941. He married Mae Missiner in 1905.

    v.   ETHEL LEONA THORNTON was born on 20 Oct 1891. She died on 27 Dec 1908. She married JAMES MARVIN CARR.

    vi.   LILLIAN LUCY THORNTON was born on 26 Aug 1896. She died in 1977. She married NAITH WOODS.

38.   **ELIZABETH LUCINDA**[4] **THORNTON** (Mary Anna[3] Garland, Peter[2] Garland, Peter[1] Garland) was born on 29 Aug 1859 in Texas. She died on 15 Mar 1948 in San Angelo, Texas. She married **HENRY C. WYLIE**.

Henry C. Wylie and Elizabeth Lucinda Thornton had the following children:

      i.   DANIEL KELSEY[5] WYLIE.

      ii.   HENRY CLAY WYLIE.

      iii.   JEWELL WYLIE.

      iv.   MATTIE WYLIE.

      v.   MODENIA WYLIE.

39.   **HENRY CLAY**[4] **THORNTON** (Mary Anna[3] Garland, Peter[2] Garland, Peter[1] Garland) was born on 09 Sep 1865 in Erath County, Texas. He died on 27 Sep 1930 in McKinney, Texas. He married Frances Bell Kenny on 05 Aug 1885.

More About Henry Clay Thornton:
Burial: 28 Sep 1930 in Breckenridge, Texas
Cause Of Death: Sarcoma
Occupation: Sheriff

Henry Clay Thornton and Frances Bell Kenny had the following children:

      i.   MINNIE LEE[5] THORNTON. She died in 1934. She married THAD ATOR.

      ii.   CLYTIE THORNTON was born on 27 Mar 1886. Clytie died on 22 May 1886.

      iii.   ODIE T. THORNTON was born on 02 Nov 1888. He married Clara Gibson on 22 Sep 1909.

      iv.   HENRY CLAYTON THORNTON was born on 24 Sep 1890. He died on 17 May 1968. He married Lester Lee Sechrist on 12 Jan 1909.

      v.   ALLYNE T. THORNTON was born on 06 Jun 1892. She died in 1972. She married Tom Bridges on 02 Oct 1913.

      vi.   ROBERT THOMAS THORNTON was born on 10 Mar 1894. He died in Sep 1932. He married Rittie Sechrist on 17 Nov 1911.

      vii. VERA FERN THORNTON was born on 08 Jul 1898. She died in 1978. She married Mack Welch on 30 May 1917.

      viii. WYLIE GARLAND THORNTON was born on 06 Sep 1901. He married Flora Blakeley in Jan 1927.

40.   **WILLIAM LUTHER**[4] **THORNTON** (Mary Anna[3] Garland, Peter[2] Garland, Peter[1] Garland) was born on 11 Dec 1866 in Erath County, Texas. He died on 29 Mar 1928 in Breckenridge, Texas. He married **JACKIE MAY KENNEDY**. She was born on 29 Dec 1871 in Anderson, Texas. She died on 06 Jul 1956 in Sherman, Texas.

More About William Luther Thornton:
Burial: 30 Mar 1928 in Breckenridge Cemetery, Breckenridge, Texas
Occupation: Hotel Propietor

More About Jackie May Kennedy:
Burial: Breckenridge Cemetery, Breckenridge, Texas

William Luther Thornton and Jackie May Kennedy had the following children:

    i.   MINNIE ORENA[5] THORNTON was born on 23 Sep 1892. She died on 09 Nov 1969. She married Prince Kinsey on 25 Jun 1913.

    ii.   CLIVE THORNTON was born on 16 Sep 1896.

    iii.   DANIEL RAYMOND THORNTON was born on 19 Mar 1898. He died on 10 Aug 1963. He married RHODA LEWIS.

41.   **ARTHUR E.**[4] **THORNTON** (Mary Anna[3] Garland, Peter[2] Garland, Peter[1] Garland) was born on 30 Sep 1871 in Texas. He died on 02 May 1951 in Ralls, Crosby County, Texas. He married Fannie Fulkerson on 27 Nov 1891.

More About Arthur E. Thornton:
Burial: 03 May 1951 in Ralls Cemetery, Ralls, Crosby County, Texas
Cause Of Death: Coronary Thrombosis
Occupation: Blacksmith

Arthur E. Thornton and Fannie Fulkerson had the following children:

    i.   ARCHIE[5] THORNTON.

    ii.   ERNEST THORNTON.

    iii.   GOLDIE THORNTON.

    iv.   OSCAR THORNTON. He married OCTAVIA (UNKNOWN).

    v.   WADE THORNTON. He married BESSIE DOBBS.

    vi.   TRESSIE THORNTON was born on 18 Apr 1897. She married Cloyd Skeeters on 24 Oct 1916.

42.   **DANIEL ROBERT**[4] **THORNTON** (Mary Anna[3] Garland, Peter[2] Garland, Peter[1] Garland) was born on 09 Jul 1875 in Hannibal, Erath County, Texas. He died on 12 Nov 1959 in Wharton, Wharton County, Texas. He married (1) **MARGUERITE V. BASS** on 03 Aug 1898. She died in 1918. He married **ETHEL RUTH (UNKNOWN)**.

More About Daniel Robert Thornton:
Burial: 13 Nov 1959 in City Cemetery, Wharton, Texas
Occupation: Court Bailiff

Daniel Robert Thornton and Marguerite V. Bass had the following children:

    i.   CONDA DOVEN[5] THORNTON was born on 19 Jul 1899. He married Minnie Myrtle Bowers in Jun 1922.

    ii.   MINNIE CLEORA THORNTON was born on 26 Apr 1901. She married Roscoe E. Ross on 12 Aug 1923.

    iii.   MARY ANNA THORNTON was born on 10 Nov 1902. She married Wesley T. Smith on 24 Nov 1923.

    iv.   WILLIAM BASS THORNTON was born on 02 Jan 1910. He married Wynelle Roberts in 1935.

    v.   DAN THORNTON was born on 31 Jul 1915. He died on 06 Aug 1915.

Daniel Robert Thornton and Ethel Ruth (unknown) had the following children:

    vi.   DANIEL ARTHUR THORNTON was born on 24 Apr 1924. He died on 06 Nov 1995 in Eagle Lake, Texas. He married Merle Jean Jenkins on 22 Apr 1945.

Notes for Daniel Arthur Thornton:
Social Security Death index gives April 22, 1924 as birth date.

    vii.   ETHEL FERN THORNTON was born on 24 Mar 1928. She married Robert Alvin Myers on 03 Jul 1942.

43.   **MINNIE KATHLEEN**[4] **THORNTON** (Mary Anna[3] Garland, Peter[2] Garland, Peter[1] Garland) was born on 12 Apr 1877 in Erath County, Texas. She died on 28 Jun 1968 in San Antonio, Texas. She married **WILLIAM EVERETT WRIGHT**. He was born on 20 Mar 1866 in Tennessee. He died on 18 Sep 1946 in San Antonio, Texas.

More About Minnie Kathleen Thornton:
Burial: 01 Jul 1968 in Mission Burial Park, San Antonio, Texas
Cause Of Death: Cardiac Arrest

More About William Everett Wright:
Burial: 20 Sep 1946 in Mission Burial Park, San Antonio, Texas
Cause Of Death: Chronic Myocarditis
Living In: 1900 Brownwood, Brown County, Texas
Living In: 1910 San Antonio, Texas
Occupation: Physician

William Everett Wright and Minnie Kathleen Thornton had the following child:

    i.   MINNIE KATHLEEN[5] WRIGHT. She married DEL WEFFING.

44.   **DELLA**[4] **HIGHTOWER** (Lucinda[3] Garland, Peter[2] Garland, Peter[1] Garland) was born in Jan 1878 in Hood County, Texas. She married **(UNKNOWN) MCKIERMAN**.

More About Della Hightower:
Living In: 1900 Della and her daughter, Pearl, are living with her parents in Township 14, Creek Nation, Indian Territory (present day Oklahoma)

Notes for Della Hightower:
Listed as widowed in 1900 U.S. census.

(unknown) Mckierman and Della Hightower had the following child:

i.   PEARL[5] MCKIERMAN was born in Sep 1898 in Indian Territory (present day Oklahoma).

45.   **PLEASANT GARLAND[4] THORP** (Melissa Virginia[3] Garland, Peter[2] Garland, Peter[1] Garland) was born on 14 Mar 1874 in Thorp Spring, Texas. He died on 19 Aug 1946 in Granbury, Texas. He married (1) **LOUISA M. ARRINGTON** about 1900. She was born on 12 Feb 1881 in Texas. She died on 06 Jan 1978 in Hood County, Texas.

More About Pleasant Garland Thorp:
Burial: 20 Aug 1946 in Friendship Cemetery, Hood County, Texas
Cause Of Death: Coronary Thrombosis
Living In: 1900 Justice Precinct 6, Hood County, Texas
Living In: 1910 Justice Precinct 1, Hood County, Texas
Occupation: 1918 - Farmer and Stock Raiser

More About Louisa M. Arrington:
Burial: Friendship Cemetery, Hood County, Texas

Pleasant Garland Thorp and Louisa M. Arrington had the following child:

i. JOE HENRY[5] THORP was born on 20 Mar 1901 in Hood County, Texas. He died on 03 May 1980 in Texas. He married Flora Mae Denton on 14 Jan 1924 in Hood County, Texas. She was born about 1907 in Tolar, Texas.

More About Joe Henry Thorp:
Burial: Friendship Cemetery, Hood County, Texas

46.   **LUCY B.[4] THORP** (Melissa Virginia[3] Garland, Peter[2] Garland, Peter[1] Garland) was born on 16 Dec 1883 in Texas. She died on 31 Dec 1978 in Bryan, Brazos County, Texas. She married Warner L. Thomas on 08 Sep 1902.

More About Lucy B. Thorp:
Burial: 03 Jan 1979 in Restover Memorial Park, Bryan, Texas

Warner L. Thomas and Lucy B. Thorp had the following child:

i.   JEWEL[5] THOMAS. She married FRANK IVER DAHLBERG.

47.   **HENRY LEE[4] NUTT** (Susan Avarilla[3] Garland, Peter[2] Garland, Peter[1] Garland) was born on 01 Apr 1878 in Granbury, Texas. He died on 17 Aug 1956 in Granbury, Texas. He married Euna Lee Barefoot, daughter of Lewis Barefoot and Mary Myrtle Oxier on 12 Aug 1903 in Chickasha, Oklahoma. She was born on 18 Feb 1883 in Montague, Texas. She died on 10 Dec 1975 in Granbury, Texas.

More About Henry Lee Nutt:
Burial: 18 Aug 1956 in Granbury Cemetery, Granbury, Texas
Cause Of Death: Pneumonia and Cerebral Hemorrhage
Living In: 1900 With his parents in Granbury, Texas.
Living In: 1910 Granbury, Hood County, Texas
Living In: 1920 Granbury, Hood County, Texas
Living In: 1930 Fort Worth, Tarrant County, Texas
Occupation: 1900 - Grocery Salesperson
Occupation: 1910 - Retail Groceries Merchant

Occupation: 1930 - Mill and Elevator Salesman
Occupation: 1920 - Grocery Merchant

Notes for Henry Lee Nutt:
Occupation listed on death certificate is Realtor.

More About Euna Lee Barefoot:
Burial: 11 Dec 1975 in Granbury Cemetery, Granbury, Texas
Cause Of Death: Cerebral Anoxia

Notes for Euna Lee Barefoot:
Occupation given on death certificate is retired hotel owner.

Henry Lee Nutt and Euna Lee Barefoot had the following children:

    i.   LOIS[5] NUTT was born about 1905 in Texas.

    ii.   DAVID EARL NUTT was born about 1913 in Texas.

    iii.   JOE LOUIS NUTT was born about 1915 in Texas.

48.   MARY SUE[4] NUTT (Susan Avarilla[3] Garland, Peter[2] Garland, Peter[1] Garland) was born on 22 Jan 1898 in Granbury, Texas. She died on 28 Jun 1974 in Granbury, Texas. She married (1) LOUIS EDWARD FAULKNER, son of King Hiram Faulkner and Mary Elvira Crites on 08 Aug 1916 in Granbury, Texas. He was born on 24 Nov 1895 in Oklahoma. He died on 12 Nov 1964 in Houston, Texas. She married (2) FRANK WILLIAM MEHRTEN, son of John Mehrten and Palmar Clover on 12 Jan 1947. He was born on 23 Apr 1895 in Knox, Pennsylvania. He died on 30 Sep 1965 in Dallas, Texas.

More About Mary Sue Nutt:
Burial: 30 Jun 1974 in Granbury Cemetery, Granbury,
Texas Cause Of Death: Acute Myocardial Infarction

More About Louis Edward Faulkner:
Burial: Granbury Cemetery, Granbury, Texas
Cause Of Death: Cerebral Hemorrhage
Occupation: Auto Parts Salesman

Louis Edward Faulkner and Mary Sue Nutt had the following children:

    i.   MARY LOUISE[5] FAULKNER was born on 15 Jun 1917 in Hood County, Texas. She died on 30 Jan 2001 in Granbury, Texas.

    ii.   DAVID GARLAND FAULKNER was born on 08 Jun 1919 in Hood County, Texas.

More About Frank William Mehrten:
Burial: 02 Oct 1965 in Granbury Cemetery, Granbury, Texas
Cause Of Death: Pulmonary Insufficiency
Occupation: Certified Accountant
Military Service: World War One

49.   ALLEN GARLAND[4] HALL (Salina J.[3] Garland, Edward[2] Garland, Peter[1] Garland) was born on 12 Jul 1862 in Kentucky. He died on 28 Nov 1915 in Nashville, Tennessee. He married Lillie Carter Gunn, daughter of Wesley Gunn and Martha Addie Grinter on 26 Feb 1885 in Kentucky. She was born on 02 Nov 1864 in Kentucky. She died on 08 Aug 1958 in Cadiz, Kentucky.

More About Allen Garland Hall:
Burial: Mount Olivet Cemetery, Nashville, Tennessee
Occupation: 1900 in Nashville, Tennessee; High School Teacher
Occupation: 1910 in Nashville, Tennessee; University Professor
Occupation: Dean of Vanderbilt University School of Law

Notes for Allen Garland Hall:
Dean of Law, Vanderbilt University.

More About Lillie Carter Gunn:
Burial: Mount Olivet Cemetery, Nashville, Tennessee

More About Allen Garland Hall and Lillie Carter Gunn:
Marriage Fact: Ceremony performed by Reverend V. Elgin

Allen Garland Hall and Lillie Carter Gunn had the following children:

  i. GLENN ANDREWS[5] HALL was born on 24 Nov 1885 in Tennessee. He died on 23 May 1953 in Tennessee.

    More About Glenn Andrews Hall:
    Living In: 1910 Living with his parents in Nashville, Tennessee.
    Occupation: 1910 in Nashville, Tennessee; Newspaper Editor
    Military Service: U. S. Marine Corps, World War One

  ii. FITZGERALD HALL was born on 06 Dec 1889 in Nashville, Tennessee. He died on 07 Feb 1946 in Nashville, Tennessee. He married ELIZABETH MURPHY GARDNER.

    More About Fitzgerald Hall:
    Occupation: President of Nashville, Chattanooga and St. Louis Railroad
    Occupation: Assistant United States District Attorney
    Occupation: Law Professor at Vanderbilt University School of Law

    Notes for Fitzgerald Hall:
    President of the Nashville, Chattanooga and Saint Louis Railroad.

50. JOSEPH EDWARD[4] GARLAND (Edward Warren[3], Edward[2], Peter[1]) was born on 17 Mar 1878 in Red River County, Texas. He died on 01 Sep 1946 in Lamesa, Dawson County, Texas. He married Lou Ethel Bynum, daughter of Alfred Baker Bynum and Dorinda Sandal Baird on 21 May 1908 in Brownfield, Texas. She was born on 25 Apr 1890 in Whitewright, Grayson County, Texas. She died on 17 Sep 1969 in Lamesa, Dawson County, Texas.

More About Joseph Edward Garland:
Burial: 03 Sep 1946 in Lamesa Cemetery, Lamesa,
Texas Cause Of Death: Cerebral Hemorrhage
Living In: 1900 With his mother and siblings in Bowie County, Texas
Occupation: 1900 in Commissioner Precinct 3, Bowie County, Texas; Day Laborer
Occupation: 1910 in Dawson County, Texas; Lawyer
Occupation: 1918 in Lamesa, Texas; County Judge and Attorney
Occupation: 1920 in Lamesa, Texas; Attorney at Law

Occupation: 1930 in Lamesa, Texas; Independent Lawyer
Occupation: 1940 in Lamesa, Texas; Attorney at Law
Military Service: Spanish American War

More About Lou Ethel Bynum:
Burial: 19 Sep 1969 in Lamesa Cemetery, Lamesa, Texas
Cause Of Death: Heart Disease

Joseph Edward Garland and Lou Ethel Bynum had the following children:

    i. EDWARD BYNUM[5] GARLAND was born on 15 Jun 1909 in Texas. He died on 30 Oct 1986 in Seminole, Texas.

       More About Edward Bynum Garland:
       Burial: Lamesa Cemetery, Lamesa, Texas
       Living In: 1930 Living with his parents in Lamesa, Texas
       Living In: 1940 Living with his parents in Lamesa, Texas
       Occupation: 1940 in Lamesa, Dawson County, Texas; Stock Farmer
       Military Service: Bet. 05 Sep 1942-15 Nov 1945; U.S. Army, World War Two

   ii.   MARGARET DORINDA GARLAND was born on 01 Oct 1911 in Lamesa, Dawson County, Texas. She died on 29 Apr 2005 in Lubbock, Texas. She married James Mack Noble, son of James Mack Noble and Rosia Lee Carter on 01 Jan 1933 in Lamesa, Texas. He was born on 29 Jun 1898 in Texas. He died on 07 Sep 1961 in O'Donnell, Texas.

       More About Margaret Dorinda Garland:
       Burial: 03 May 2005 in O'Donnell Cemetery, O'Donnell, Texas

       Notes for Margaret Dorinda Garland:
         Lubbock Avalanche-Journal
       Obituary of Margaret Garland Noble
       Published: Monday, May 02, 2005

       Margaret Garland Noble, 93, of Lubbock and formerly of ODonnell died Friday, April 29, 2005 at Grace House in Lubbock. She was born Sept. 30, 1911 in Lamesa. She married James Mack Noble, Jr. Jan. 1, 1933 in Lamesa. He preceded her in death in 1961.

       Mrs. Noble was the daughter of Joseph Edward and Ethel Garland, who were early pioneer settlers in Dawson and Lynn counties. She was a world traveler, seeing places like China, Australia, New Zealand and Central America. In 1981, she and her family traveled to Scandinavia and Russia.

       Margaret was employed by the U.S. Postal Service as a mail carrier. She belonged to Tuesday Bridge and Study Club in ODonnell.

       Two brothers, James and Edward, also precede her in death.

       Survivors include: two sons, Edward Garland of San Francisco Bay Area, Calif. and James Mack, III of Longview; two grandchildren; and two great-grandchildren.

       Services will be 4 p.m. Tuesday at First United Methodist Church in ODonnell with the Rev. Kenneth Peterson officiating.

Burial will be in ODonnell Cemetery.

The family suggests memorial to the ODonnell Cemetery Association or a charity of choice.

Birth date is from birth certificate.

----

  iii. JAMES GARLAND was born on 20 Sep 1918 in Lamesa, Dawson County, Texas. He died on 25 Feb 1988 in Hobbs, New Mexico. He married (1) EVA MAE WATERS on 01 Jun 1950 in Dawson County, Texas. She was born about 1924. He married DOROTHY (UNKNOWN).

    More About James Garland:
    Burial: Dawson County Cemetery, Lamesa, Dawson County, Texas
    Occupation: 1940 in Honolulu, Hawaii Territory; Medical Department, Tripler General Hospital, U.S. Army
    Military Service: Bet. 1940-1945; World War Two

    Notes for James Garland:
    Present during Japanese attack on Pearl Harbor, December 7, 1941.
    Served in Europe- Normandy to V.E. Day.
    Divorced from Eva Waters on January 16, 1974 in Gaines County, Texas.

51. **EMMA GEORGIE IRENE**[4] **GARLAND** (Edward Warren[3], Edward[2], Peter[1]) was born on 23 Mar 1880 in Annona, Texas. She died on 17 Dec 1969 in Kerrville, Texas. She married LeRoy Ardis Edwards in May 1921 in Roscoe, Texas. He was born on 27 Feb 1881 in Sulphur Springs, Texas. He died on 05 Dec 1951 in Loraine, Texas.

More About Emma Georgie Irene Garland:
Burial: 20 Dec 1969 in Loraine Cemetery, Loraine, Texas
Cause Of Death: Broncho Pneumonia and Arteriosclerosis
Living In: 1920 Lamesa, Texas with sister Estelle and family.
Occupation: 1920 in Lamesa, Texas; Teacher

More About LeRoy Ardis Edwards:
Burial: 07 Dec 1951 in Loraine Cemetery, Loraine, Texas
Cause Of Death: Carcinoma of Lung
Occupation: 1930 in Loraine, Texas; Lumber Yard Manager
Occupation: 1940 in Olton, Texas; Retail Lumber Yard Manager

Notes for LeRoy Ardis Edwards:
Discovered and owned, with his brother Walter, "Baking Powder" gold mine in New Mexico.

LeRoy Ardis Edwards and Emma Georgie Irene Garland had the following child:

  i. ROY GARLAND[5] EDWARDS was born on 30 May 1922 in Loraine, Texas. He died on 14 Oct 1974 in Tampa, Florida. He married Maribel Savage on 08 Apr 1944 in Lubbock, Texas. She was born on 22 Jun 1926 in Sherman, texas. She died on 14 Feb 2010 in Tampa, Florida.

    More About Roy Garland Edwards:
    Burial: Pleasant Grove Cemetery, Durant, Florida

Cause Of Death: Heart Failure
Military Service: Bet. 1942-1964; U.S. Air Force (Major)

52. MAGGIE AUGUSTA ESTELLE[4] GARLAND (Edward Warren[3], Edward[2], Peter[1]) was born in Aug 1884 in DeKalb, Texas. She died on 29 Jan 1955 in Sweetwater, Texas. She married Barna Haney, son of William Daniel Haney and Mamie H. Harkins on 24 May 1911 in Roscoe, Texas. He was born on 30 Nov 1887 in Temple, Bell County, Texas. He died on 27 Jan 1957 in Roscoe, Texas.

More About Maggie Augusta Estelle Garland:
Burial: 31 Jan 1955 in Roscoe Cemetery, Roscoe, Texas
Cause Of Death: Cerebral Hemorhage
Living In: 1910 Living with her brother, Rufus Garland, in Roscoe, Texas
Living In: 1920 Lamesa, Texas
Living In: 1930 Roscoe, Texas
Living In: 1955 Roscoe, Texas
Occupation: 1910 in Roscoe, Texas; Dry Goods Saleslady

More About Barna Haney:
Burial: 28 Jan 1957 in Roscoe Cemetery, Roscoe,
Texas
Living In: 1900 Bell County, Texas
Living In: 1910 Living with his parents in Roscoe, Texas
Occupation: 1910 in Roscoe, Texas; Furniture Sales Clerk
Occupation: 1920 in Lamesa, Texas; Clerk in Meyers Drug Company
Occupation: 1930 in Roscoe, Texas; Druggist in Drug Store
Occupation: 1932 in Roscoe, Texas; President of Board of Education
Occupation: 1940 in Roscoe, Texas; Pharmacist and Drug Store owner, Roscoe, Texas

Notes for Barna Haney:
Owned Haney Drug Store, Roscoe, Texas. Mayor and School Board Member of Roscoe, Texas.

More About Barna Haney and Maggie Augusta Estelle Garland:
Marriage License: 23 May 1911 in Nolan County, Texas
Marriage Fact: Married by Rev. J. W. Smith, M. E. Church South, Roscoe, Texas.

Barna Haney and Maggie Augusta Estelle Garland had the following children:

 i. WILLIAM GARLAND[5] HANEY was born on 11 May 1912 in Roscoe, Texas. He died on 19 Jan 1988 in Lubbock, Texas. He married Allie Pearl Dunn, daughter of Yanks Dunn and Ada Branson on 04 Oct 1942 in Roscoe, Texas. She was born on 07 Oct 1922 in Burleson, Texas. She died on 29 Apr 2007 in Roscoe, Texas.

More About William Garland Haney:
Burial: Roscoe Cemetery, Roscoe, Texas
Living In: 1940 Living with his parents in Roscoe, Texas
Occupation: 1940 in Roscoe, Texas; Retail Drug Clerk
Occupation: Pharmacist
Military Service: Enlisted at Lubbock, Texas, January 15, 1942 in U.S. Army for World War Two

Notes for William Garland Haney:
Held rank of SSgt. while in U.S. Army.

 ii.   MARY JULIA HANEY was born on 16 Aug 1916. She died on 25 Jun 1996 in

Clarkesville, Texas. She married Joseph Dellinger Garland, son of Wirt Robert Garland and Lola Prudence Dellinger on 21 Jun 1942 in Roscoe, Texas. He was born on 07 Dec 1914 in Annona, Texas. He died on 16 Aug 1973 in Clarkesville, Texas.

More About Mary Julia Haney:
Burial: 29 Jun 1996 in Garland Cemetery, Annona, Texas
Living In: 1940 Living with her parents in Roscoe, Texas.
Occupation: 1940 in Roscoe, Texas; Music Teacher
Occupation: Music Teacher, Pianist, Organist

53. **MATTHEW LENORE[4] WALSH** (Martha A. Elizabeth[3] Garland, Thomas Lowery[2] Garland, Peter[1] Garland) was born on 08 Mar 1874 in Arkansas. He died on 04 Nov 1903 in Stamps, Arkansas. He married Mabel May Lowe, daughter of Millard Lowe and Julia Knowlen on 17 Nov 1900 in Corning, Arkansas.

More About Matthew Lenore Walsh:
Cause Of Death: Bled to death after his legs were severed by a train.

Matthew Lenore Walsh and Mabel May Lowe had the following child:

    i.   MARTHA JULIA[5] WALSH was born on 18 Sep 1901 in Conway, Arkansas. She died on 26 Apr 1982 in San Antonio, Texas. She married Simeon Elijah Tyler, son of William Henry Tyler and Mary Pugh on 26 May 1921 in New Orleans, Louisiana. He was born on 04 Jul 1891.

54. **BONNIE EARL[4] GARLAND** (Joseph Daniel[3], Thomas Lowery[2], Peter[1]) was born on 29 Nov 1871 in near Bradford, White County, Arkansas. She died on 11 Aug 1959 in Higo, Choctaw County, Oklahoma. She married Thomas Wright on 05 Feb 1888 in Polk County, Arkansas. He was born about 1860 in Tennessee.

Thomas Wright and Bonnie Earl Garland had the following children:

    i.   JAMES[5] WRIGHT was born on 31 Dec 1888 in Arkansas. He died on 16 Apr 1968 in Choctaw County, Oklahoma.

    ii.   HALDER WRIGHT.

    iii.   HULBERT WRIGHT.

    iv.   ETHEL WRIGHT.

    v.   JACIA WRIGHT.

    vi.   LODIE WRIGHT.

    vii.   GEORGE WRIGHT.

55. **LILLIE THOMAS[4] WINSTON** (Margaret C.[3] Garland, John Calhoun[2] Garland, Peter[1] Garland) was born on 08 Dec 1858 in Bowe County, Texas. She died on 04 Aug 1938 in Red River County, Texas. She married **THOMAS JEFFERSON LAWSON**. He was born on 27 Feb 1849 in Texas. He died on 06 Apr 1887 in Texas.

More About Lillie Thomas Winston:
Burial: 05 Aug 1938 in Garland Cemetery, Red River County, Texas
Living In: 1900 Lillie and her children living at her parents' home in Red River County, Texas

Notes for Lillie Thomas Winston:
Headstone has December 9, 1858 for date of birth. Death certificate has December 8, 1858
for date of birth.

More About Thomas Jefferson Lawson:
Burial: Garland Cemetery, Red River County, Texas
Occupation: Farmer

Thomas Jefferson Lawson and Lillie Thomas Winston had the following children:

    i. OSCAR C.[5] LAWSON was born on 01 Feb 1877 in Texas. He died on 05 Aug 1932 in San
        Antonio, Texas. He married DORAH (UNKNOWN).

        More About Oscar C. Lawson:
        Burial: Garland Cemetery, Annona, Texas
        Cause Of Death: Cerebral Hemorrhage
        Occupation: 1900; Teacher, Red River County, Texas
        Occupation: 1932, Insurance salesman

        Notes for Oscar C. Lawson:
        Headstone has February 7, 1877 for date of birth. Death certificate has February
        1, 1877 for date of birth. Headstone has August 4, 1932 for date of death. Death
        certificate has August 5, 1932 for date of death.

    ii. WALTER SCOTT LAWSON was born on 11 Nov 1878 in Annona, Texas. He died on
        04 Dec 1949 in Red River County, Texas.

        More About Walter Scott Lawson:
        Burial: 06 Dec 1949 in Garland Cemetery, Annona, Texas
        Occupation: 1900; Farmer, Red River County, Texas

    iii. ELLA L. LAWSON was born on 21 Aug 1883 in Texas. She died on 03 Jan 1948
        in Fort Worth, Texas. She married (UNKNOWN) ANDERSON.

        More About Ella L. Lawson:
        Burial: 05 Jan 1948 in Greenwood Cemetery, Fort Worth,
        Texas Cause Of Death: Carcinoma of Uterus
        Occupation: 1900 - Literary Student

    iv. THOMAS J. LAWSON was born in Sep 1886 in Texas.

        More About Thomas J. Lawson:
        Occupation: 1900 - Farm Labor

56. JOELLA G.[4] GARLAND (Joseph Daniel Ramey[3], John Calhoun[2], Peter[1]) was born on 02 Apr 1878 in
Annona, Texas. She died on 22 Mar 1946 in Clarkesville, Texas. She married (1) JOHN R. PEEK on 18
Feb 1903 in Red River County, Texas. He was born on 09 Oct 1877. He died on 08 Nov 1909.

She married **JOHN HIRAM DOOLEY**. He was born on 24 Jul 1870 in Lamar County, Texas. He died on 28 May 1951 in Sherman, Texas.

More About Joella G. Garland:
Burial: 24 Mar 1946 in Garland Cemetery, Red River County, Texas
Cause Of Death: Coronary Thrombosis and Acute Myocardial Failure

More About John R. Peek:
Burial: Garland Cemetery, Red River County, Texas

John R. Peek and Joella G. Garland had the following child:

       i. JOHN R.[5] PEEK was born on 17 Nov 1904 in Texas. He died on 22 Jan 1968 in San Antonio, Texas.

          More About John R. Peek:
          Burial: 24 Jan 1938 in Rosemound Cemetery, Waco, Texas
          Cause Of Death: Amistrophic Lateral Sclerosis

More About John Hiram Dooley:
Burial: Garland Cemetery, Red River County, Texas
Burial:
Cause Of Death: Acute Pulmonary Edema
Occupation: Peace Officer

John Hiram Dooley and Joella G. Garland had the following child:

       i.   JACK W.[5] DOOLEY was born in 1917. He died in 1964.

          More About Jack W. Dooley:
          Burial: Garland Cemetery, Red River County, Texas

57.   **MARY LEDA[4] GARLAND** (Joseph Daniel Ramey[3], John Calhoun[2], Peter[1]) was born on 20 Jan 1880 in Annona, Texas. She died on 18 Oct 1967 in Sherman, Texas. She married **JOSEPH B. WRIGHT**. He was born on 19 Dec 1887 in Grenada, Mississippi. He died on 21 Jan 1967 in Sherman, Texas.

More About Mary Leda Garland:
Burial: 19 Oct 1967 in Garland Cemetery, Red River County, Texas Cause Of Death: Multiple Cerebro Vascular Thrombosis

More About Joseph B. Wright:
Burial: 23 Jan 1967 in Garland Cemetery, Red River County, Texas Cause Of Death: Acute Myocardial Infarction
Occupation: Hotel Clerk

Notes for Joseph B. Wright:
Headstone and Social Security death index have December 19, 1887 for date of birth. Death certificate has December 20, 1887 for date of birth.

Joseph B. Wright and Mary Leda Garland had the following child:

       i.   THOMAS GARLAND[5] WRIGHT was born on 30 Sep 1910. He died on 30 Sep 1910.

More About Thomas Garland Wright:
Burial: Garland Cemetery, Red River County, Texas

58.   **WIRT ROBERT**[4] **GARLAND** (Joseph Daniel Ramey[3], John Calhoun[2], Peter[1]) was born on 31 Mar 1881 in Annona, Texas. He died on 18 May 1963 in Texarkana, Texas. He married Lola Prudence Dellinger, daughter of Charles F. Dellinger and Sarah Eaker in 1902 in Annona, Texas. She was born on 03 Aug 1881 in Annona, Texas. She died on 19 Feb 1969 in Clarkesville, Texas.

More About Wirt Robert Garland:
b: 31 Mar 1881
Burial: 20 May 1963 in Garland Cemetery, Red River County,
Texas
Living In: 1963 in Annona, Texas
Occupation: Farmer and Cattleman

More About Lola Prudence Dellinger:
b: 03 Aug 1881
Burial: 21 Feb 1969 in Garland Cemetery, Red River County, Texas
Cause Of Death: Malignant Lymphoma

Wirt Robert Garland and Lola Prudence Dellinger had the following children:

     i. ERA LEDA[5] GARLAND was born on 25 Jul 1904 in Annona, Texas. She died on 16 Aug 1904 in Annona, Texas.

       More About Era Leda Garland:
       Burial: Garland Cemetery, Red River County, Texas

    ii.   MARY DELLA ELIZABETH GARLAND was born on 31 Jul 1906 in Annona, Texas. She died on 05 Mar 1993 in Minneapolis, Minnesota. She married Wallace David Armstrong on 19 Aug 1929 in Annona, Texas. He was born on 08 Jul 1905 in Hickory Creek, Texas. He died on 07 Jun 1984 in St. Paul, Minnesota.

       More About Mary Della Elizabeth Garland:
       Burial: 09 Mar 1993 in Garland Cemetery, Annona, Texas

    iii. WIRT RUSSELL GARLAND was born on 31 Oct 1909 in Annona, Texas. He died on 22 May 1947 in Fort Sam Houston, Texas. He married Nancy Rhine Maxfield in May 1937.

       More About Wirt Russell Garland:
       Burial: 24 May 1947 in Garland Cemetery, Red River County,
       Texas Cause Of Death: ; Congestive Heart Failure
       Occupation: ; Draftsman
       Military Service: ; U. S. Army, World War Two, Enlisted October 12, 1942

    iv.   JOSEPH DELLINGER GARLAND was born on 07 Dec 1914 in Annona, Texas. He died on 16 Aug 1973 in Clarkesville, Texas. He married Mary Julia Haney, daughter of Barna Haney and Maggie Augusta Estelle Garland on 21 Jun 1942 in Roscoe, Texas. She was born on 16 Aug 1916. She died on 25 Jun 1996 in Clarkesville, Texas.

       More About Joseph Dellinger Garland:

b: 07 Dec 1914
Burial: 18 Aug 1973 in Garland Cemetery, Annona,
Texas
Cause Of Death: Acute Myocardial Infarction
Occupation: Banker
Occupation: Welfare Agent
Military Service: SSgt., United States army

    v.   LILLIAN INEZ GARLAND was born on 25 Dec 1915 in Annona, Texas. She died in Oct 1999. She married WILLIAM EDGAR NOWLIN.

59.   **ROY LATIMER[4] GARLAND** (Joseph Daniel Ramey[3], John Calhoun[2], Peter[1]) was born on 05 Apr 1892 in Annona, Texas. He died on 01 May 1968 in Texarkana, Bowie County, Texas. He married Mamie Claire Pipkin, daughter of Thomas P. Pipkin and Mollie Gaines in Kaufman, Texas. She was born on 19 Mar 1891. She died on 07 Nov 1957 in Clarkesville, Texas.

More About Roy Latimer Garland:
Burial: 03 May 1968 in Garland Cemetery, Red River County,
Texas
Cause Of Death: Myocardial Infarction
Living In: 1968 Annona, Texas
Occupation: Rancher

More About Mamie Claire Pipkin:
Burial: 10 Nov 1957 in Garland Cemetery, Red River County,
Texas Cause Of Death: Hypertensive Heart Disease

Roy Latimer Garland and Mamie Claire Pipkin had the following child:

    i.   GLENDA[5] GARLAND was born about 1915. She died about 1965. She married WILLIAM YOUNGBLOOD.

60.   **JAMES POLK[4] GARLAND** (Ruth[3], John Calhoun[2], Peter[1]) was born about 1848. He married **J. (UNKNOWN)**. She was born about 1858.

James Polk Garland and J. (unknown) had the following children:

    i.   LAURA[5] GARLAND. She married (UNKNOWN).

    ii.   EFFIE GARLAND was born about 1877.

    iii.   SMITHY GARLAND.

    iv.   JOSEPH GARLAND was born about 1879.